The Author and her sons.

WOMAN AND THE NEW RACE

BY

MARGARET SANGER

[1920]

Republished By;

2011
Moorthings Inc
PO Box 701
Heath Springs SC 29058

Moorthings@yahoo.com

Margaret Sanger wrote this book in 1920 at the high water mark of the first wave of feminism. Women in the United States could now vote, own property, acquire higher education, and many other rights won through hard struggle. Sanger saw a woman's right to control her own body (specifically her reproductive system) as the next big goal. It took more than forty years before a new wave of feminism, along with advances in medical technology, made this attainable.

Of course, this is still the fault-line which runs through the topic of women and religion. The themes which Sanger raises in this book still arouse vehement debate, and pertain to contemporary issues which would have seemed unimaginable to Sanger, such as human cloning and stem-cell research.

Some of the language in this book may mystify or confuse contemporary readers. When she speaks of a 'New Race' she means the improvement of the human species in general. She occasionally uses arguments similar to the Eugenics movement (which was later embraced by the Nazis). This has been used as ammunition by some opposed to women's reproductive rights, and several misleading quotes either taken out of context or completely fabricated have been attributed to her in an attempt to demonize her. This is a disservice and dishonors Sangers' legacy.

Sanger later denounced the Eugenics movement. Her books were among the first burned by the Nazis. She also personally helped several Jewish women and men escape Nazi Germany. Sanger was about as far from a reactionary as could be imagined--note her opposition to militarism, her ardent feminism and activism on behalf of working-class women, her support for labor and the rights of immigrants, all of which she makes clear in this book. She opened clinics in Harlem to bring health services to the African American community, and worked closely with such African American activists as W.E.B. DuBois and Adam Clayton Powell. In 1966, the year Sanger died, the Rev. Martin Luther King, Jr. said:

There is a striking kinship between our movement and Margaret Sanger's early efforts. . . . Our sure beginning in the struggle for equality by nonviolent direct action may not have been so resolute without the tradition established by Margaret Sanger and people like her.

Sanger's opposition to abortion has to be considered in the light of the reality of pre-Roe v. Wade 'back-alley' abortion, which often had fatal or harmful side-effects. She states that she would not be opposed to abortion if it could be performed safely.

Sangers' transcendent (and very spiritual) vision of women and humanity in general free from the shackles of sexual repression and endless child-bearing is impressive, and overwhelms the shortcomings of this book. -- *jbh*

CONTENTS

WOMAN AND THE NEW RACE

CHAPTER I

WOMAN'S ERROR AND HER DEBT

THE most far-reaching social development of modern times is the revolt of woman against sex servitude. The most important force in the remaking of the world is a free motherhood. Beside this force, the elaborate international programmers of modern statesmen are weak and superficial. Diplomats may formulate leagues of nations and nations may pledge their utmost strength to maintain them, statesmen may dream of reconstructing the world out of alliances, hegemonies and spheres of influence, but woman, continuing to produce explosive populations, will convert these pledges into the proverbial scraps of paper; or she may, by controlling birth, lift motherhood to the plane of a voluntary, intelligent function, and remake the world. When the world is thus remade, it will exceed the dream of statesman, reformer and revolutionist.

Only in recent years has woman's position as the gentler and weaker half of the human family been emphatically and generally questioned. Men assumed that this was woman's place; woman herself accepted it. It seldom occurred to anyone to ask whether she would go on occupying it forever.

Upon the mere surface of woman's organized protests there were no indications that she was desirous of achieving a fundamental change in her position. She claimed the right of suffrage and legislative regulation of her working hours, and asked that her property rights be equal to those of the man. None of these demands, however, affected directly the most vital factors of her existence. Whether she won her point or failed to win it, she remained a dominated weakling in a society controlled by men.

Woman's acceptance of her inferior status was the more real because it was unconscious. She had chained herself to her place in society and the family through the maternal functions of her nature, and only chains thus strong could have bound her to her lot as a brood animal for the masculine civilizations of the world. In accepting her rôle as the "weaker and gentler half," she accepted that function. In turn, the acceptance of that function fixed the more firmly her rank as an inferior.

Caught in this "vicious circle," woman has, through her reproductive ability, founded and perpetuated the tyrannies of the Earth. Whether it was the tyranny of a monarchy, an oligarchy or a republic, the one indispensable factor of its existence was, as it is now, hordes of human beings--human beings so plentiful as to be cheap, and so cheap that ignorance was their natural lot. Upon the rock of an unenlightened, submissive maternity have these been founded; upon the product of such a maternity have they flourished.

No despot ever flung forth his legions to die in foreign conquest, no privilege-ruled nation ever erupted across its borders, to lock in death embrace with another, but behind them loomed the driving power of a population too large for its boundaries and its natural resources.

No period of low wages or of idleness with their want among the workers, no peonage or sweatshop, no child-labor factory, ever came into being, save from the same source. Norhave famine and plague been as much "acts of God" as acts of too prolific mothers. They, also, as all students know, have their basic causes in over-population.

The creators of over-population are the women, who, while wringing their hands over each fresh horror, submit anew to their task of producing the multitudes who will bring about the next tragedy of civilization.

While unknowingly laying the foundations of tyrannies and providing the human tinder for racial conflagrations, woman was also unknowingly creating slums, filling asylums with insane, and institutions with other defectives. She was replenishing the ranks of the prostitutes, furnishing grist for the criminal courts and inmates for prisons. Had she planned deliberately to achieve this tragic total of human waste and misery, she could hardly have done it more effectively.

Woman's passivity under the burden of her disastrous task was almost altogether that of ignorant resignation. She knew virtually nothing about her reproductive nature and less about the consequences of her excessive childbearing. It is true that, obeying the inner urge of their natures, *some* women revolted. They went even to the extreme of infanticide and abortion. Usually their revolts were not general enough. They fought as individuals, not as a mass. In the mass they sank back into blind and hopeless subjection. They went on breeding with staggering rapidity those numberless, undesired children who become the clogs and the destroyers of civilizations.

To-day, however, woman is rising in fundamental revolt. Even her efforts at mere reform are, as we shall see later, steps in that direction. Underneath each of them is the feminine urge to complete freedom. Millions of women are asserting their right to voluntary motherhood. They are determined to decide for themselves whether they shall become mothers, under what conditions and when. This is the fundamental revolt referred to. It is for woman the key to the temple of liberty.

Even as birth control is the means by which woman attains basic freedom, so it is the means by which she must and will uproot the evil she has wrought through her submission. As she has unconsciously and ignorantly brought about social disaster, so must and will she consciously and intelligently *undo* that disaster and create a new and a better order.

The task is hers. It cannot be avoided by excuses, nor can it be delegated. It is not enough for woman to point to the self-evident domination of man. Nor does it avail to plead the guilt of rulers and the exploiters of labor. It makes no difference that she does not formulate industrial systems nor that she is an instinctive believer in social justice. In her submission lies her error and her guilt. By her failure to withhold the multitudes of children who have made inevitable the most flagrant of our social evils, she incurred a debt to society. Regardless of her own wrongs, regardless of her lack of opportunity and regardless of all other considerations, she must pay that debt.

She must not think to pay this debt in any superficial way. She cannot pay it with palliatives--
with child-labor laws, prohibition, regulation of prostitution and agitation against war. Political
nostrums and social panaceas are but incidentally and superficially useful. They do not touch the
source of the social disease. War, famine, poverty and oppression of the workers will continue
while woman makes life cheap. They will cease only when she limits her reproductive and
human life is no longer a thing to be wasted.

Two chief obstacles binder the discharge of this tremendous obligation. The first and the lesser is
the legal barrier. Dark-Age laws would still deny to her the knowledge of her reproductive
nature. Such knowledge is indispensable to intelligent motherhood and she must achieve it,
despite absurd statutes and equally absurd moral canons.

The second and more serious barrier is her own ignorance of the extent and effect of her
submission. Until she knows the evil her subjection has wrought to herself, to her progeny and to
the world at large, she cannot wipe out that evil.

To get rid of these obstacles is to invite attack from the forces of reaction which are so strongly
entrenched in our present-day society. It means warfare in every phase of her life. Nevertheless,
at whatever cost, she must emerge from her ignorance and assume her responsibility. She can do
this only when she has awakened to a knowledge of herself and of the consequences of her
ignorance. The first step is birth control. Through birth control she will attain to voluntary
motherhood. Having attained this, the basic freedom of her sex, she will cease to enslave herself
and the mass of humanity. Then, through the understanding of the intuitive forward urge within
her, she will not stop at patching up the world; she will remake it.

CHAPTER II

WOMAN'S STRUGGLE FOR FREEDOM

BEHIND all customs of whatever nature; behind all social unrest, behind all movements, behind
all revolutions, are great driving forces, which in their action and reaction upon conditions, give
character to civilization. If, in seeking to discover the source of a custom, of a movement or of a
revolution, we stop at surface conditions, we shall never discern more than a superficial aspect of
the underlying truth.

This is the error into which the historian has almost universally fallen. It is also a common error
among sociologists. It is the fashion nowadays, for instance, to explain all social unrest in terms
of economic conditions. This is a valuable working theory and has done much to awaken men to
their injustice toward one another, but it ignores the forces *within* humanity which drive it to
revolt. It is these forces, rather than the conditions upon which they react, that are the important
factors. Conditions change, but the animating force goes on forever.

So, too, with woman's struggle for emancipation. Women in all lands and all ages have
instinctively desired family limitation. Usually this desire has been laid to economic pressure.
Frequently the pressure has existed, but the driving force behind woman's aspiration *toward*

freedom has lain deeper. It has asserted itself among the rich and among the poor, among the intelligent and the unintelligent. It has been manifested in such horrors as infanticide, child abandonment and abortion.

The only term sufficiently comprehensive to define this motive power of woman's nature is the *feminine spirit*. That spirit manifests itself most frequently in motherhood, but it is greater than maternity. Woman herself, all that she is, all that she has ever been, all that she may be, is but the outworking of this inner spiritual urge. Given free play, this supreme law of her nature asserts itself in beneficent ways; interfered with, it becomes destructive. Only when we understand this can we comprehend the efforts of the feminine spirit to liberate itself.

When the outworking of this force within her is hampered by the bearing and the care of too many children, woman rebels. Hence it is that, from time immemorial, she has sought some form of family limitation. When she has not employed such measures consciously, she has done so instinctively. Mere laws, customs and religious restrictions do not prevent, she has recourse to contraceptives. Otherwise, she resorts to child abandonment, abortion and infanticide, or resigns herself hopelessly to enforced maternity.

These violent means of freeing herself from the chains of her own reproductivity have been most in evidence where economic conditions have made the care of children even more of a burden than it would otherwise have been. But, whether in the luxurious home of the Athenian, the poverty-ridden dwelling of the Chinese, or the crude hut of the primitive Australian savage, the woman whose development has been interfered with by the bearing and rearing of children has tried desperately, frantically, too often in vain, to take and hold her freedom.

Individual men have sometimes acquiesced in these violent measures, but in the mass they have opposed. By law, by religious canons, by public opinion, by penalties ranging all the way from ostracism to beheading, they have sought to crush this effort. Neither threat of hell nor the infliction of physical punishment has availed. Women have deceived and dared, resisted and defied the power of church and state. Quietly, desperately, consciously, they have marched to the gates of death to gain the liberty which the feminine spirit has desired.

In savage life as well as in barbarism and civilization has woman's instinctive urge to freedom and a wider development asserted itself in an effort, successful or otherwise, to curtail her family.

"The custom of infanticide prevails or has prevailed," says Westermark in his monumental work, *The Origin and Development of the Moral Idea*, "not only in the savage world but among the semi-civilized and civilized races."

With the savage mother, family limitation ran largely to infanticide, although that practice was frequently accompanied by abortion as a tribal means. As McLennan says in his "Studies in Ancient History," infanticide was formerly very common among the savages of New Zealand, and "it was generally perpetrated by the mother." He notes much the same state of affairs among the primitive Australians, except that abortion was also frequently employed.. In numerous North

American Indian tribes, he says, infanticide and abortion were not uncommon, and the Indians of Central America were found by him "to have gone to extremes in the use of abortives."

'When a traveler reproached the women of one of the South American Indian tribes for the practice of infanticide, McLennan says he was met by the retort, "Men have no business to meddle with women's affairs."

McLennan ventures the opinion that the practice of abortion so widely noted among Indians in the Western Hemisphere, "must have supervened on a practice of infanticide."

Similar practices have been found to prevail wherever historians have dug deep into the life of savage people. Infanticide, at least, was practiced by African tribes, by the primitive peoples of Japan, India and Western Europe, as well as in China, and in early Greece and Rome. The ancient Hebrews are sometimes pointed out as the one possible exception to this practice, because the Mosaic law, as it has come down to us, is silent upon the subject. Westermark is of the opinion that it "hardly occurred among the Hebrews in historic times. But we have reason to believe that at an earlier period, among them, as among other branches of the Semitic race, child murder was frequently practiced as a sacrificial rite."

Westermark found that "the murder of female infants, whether by the direct employment of homicidal means, or exposure to privation and neglect, has for ages been a common practice or even a genuine custom among various Hindu castes."

Still further light is shed upon the real sources of the practice, as well as upon the improvement of the status of woman through the practice, by an English student of conditions in India. Captain S. Charles MacPherson, of the Madras Army, in the Journal of the Royal Asiatic Society for 1852, said: "I can here but very briefly advert to the customs and feelings which the practice of infanticide (among the Khonds of Orissa) alternately springs from and produces. The influence and privileges of women are exceedingly great among the Khonds, and are, I believe, greatest among the tribes which practice infanticide. Their opinions have great weight in all public an private affairs; their participation is often considered essential in the former."

If infanticide did not spring from a desire within the woman herself, from a desire stronger than motherhood, would it prevail where women enjoy an influence equal to that of men? And does not the fact that the women in question do enjoy such influence, point unmistakably to the motive behind the practice?

Infanticide did not go out of fashion with the advance from savagery to barbarism and civilization. Rather, it became, as in Greece and Rome, a recognized custom with advocates among leaders of thought and action. {p. 16} So did abortion, which some authorities regard as a development springing from infanticide and tending to supersede it as a means of getting rid of undesired children.

As progress is made toward civilization, infanticide, then, actually increased. This tendency was noted by Westermark, who also calls attention to the conclusions of Fison and Howitt (in Kamilaroi and Kurnai). "Mr. Fison who has lived for a long time among uncivilized races," says

Westermark, "thinks it will be found that infanticide is far less common among the lower savages than among the more advanced tribes."

Following this same tendency into civilized countries, we find infanticide either advocated by philosophers and authorized by law, as in Greece and Rome, or widely practiced in spite of the law, civil and ecclesiastical.

The status of infanticide as an established, legalized custom in Greece, is well summed up by Westermark, who says: "The exposure of deformed or sickly infants was undoubtedly an ancient custom in Greece; in Sparta, at least, it was enjoined by law. It was also approved of by the most enlightened among the Greek philosophers. Plato condemns all those children who are imperfect in limbs as well as those who are born of depraved citizens."

Aristotle, who believed that the state should fix the number of children each married pair should have, has this to say in *Politics*, Book, VII, Chapter V:

"With respect to the exposing and nurturing of children, let it be a law that nothing mutilated shall be nurtured. And in order to avoid having too great a number of children, if it be not permitted by the laws of the country to expose them, it is then requisite to define how many a man may have; and if any have more than the prescribed number, some means must be adopted that the fruit be destroyed in the womb of the mother before sense and life are generated in it."

Aristotle was a conscious advocate of family limitation even if attained by violent means. "It is necessary," he says, "to take care that the increase of the people should not exceed a certain number in order to avoid poverty and its concomitants, sedition and other evils."

In Athens, while the citizen wives were unable to throw off the restrictions of the laws which kept them at home, the great number of *hetera*, or stranger women, were the glory of the "Golden Age." The homes of these women who were free from the burden of too many children became the gathering places of philosophers, poets, sculptors and statesmen. The *hetera* were their companions, their inspiration and their teachers. Aspasia, one of the greatest women of antiquity, was such an emancipated individuality. True to the urge of the feminine spirit, she, like Sappho, the poetess of Lesbia, sought to arouse the Greek wives to the expression of their individual selves. One writer says of her efforts: "This woman determined to do her utmost to elevate her sex. The one method of culture open to women at that time was poetry. There was no other form of literature, and accordingly she systematically trained her pupils; to be poets, and to weave into the verse the noblest maxims of the intellect and the deepest emotions of the heart. Young pupils with richly endowed minds flocked to her from all countries and formed a kind of Woman's College.

"There can be no doubt that these young women were impelled to seek the society of Sappho from disgust with the low drudgery and monotonous routine to which woman's life was sacrificed, and they were anxious to rise to something nobler and better."

Can there be any doubt that the unfortunate "citizen wives" of Athens, bound by law to their homes envied the brilliant careers of the "stranger women," and sought all possible means of freedom? And can there be any doubt that they acquiesced in the practice of infanticide as a means to that end? Otherwise, how could the custom of destroying infants have been so thoroughly embedded in the jurisprudence, the thought and the very core of Athenian civilization?

As to the Spartan women, Aristotle says that they ruled their husbands and owned two-fifths of the land. Surely, had they not approved of infanticide for some very strong reasons of their own, they would have abolished it.

Athens and Sparta must be regarded as giving every strong indications that the Grecian women not only approved of family limitation by the destruction of unwanted children, but that at least part of their motive was personal freedom.

In Rome, an avowedly militaristic nation, living by conquest of weaker states, all sound children were saved. But the weakly, or deformed were drowned. Says Seneca: "We destroy monstrous births, and we also drown our children if they are born weakly or unnaturally formed." Wives of Romans, however, were relieved of much of the drudgery of child rearing by the slaves which Rome took by the thousands and brought home. Thus they were free to attain an advanced position and to become the advisors of their husbands in politics, making and unmaking political careers.

When we come to look into the proverbial infanticide of the Chinese, we find the same positive indications that it grew out of the instinctive purpose of woman to free herself from the bondage of too great reproductivity.

"In the poorest districts of China," says Westermark, "female infants are often destroyed by their parents immediately after their birth, chiefly on account of poverty. {p. 21} Though disapproved of by educated Chinese, the practice is treated with forebearance or indifference by the man of the people and is acquiesced in by the mandarins."

"When seriously appealed to on the subject," says the Rev. J. Doolittle in *Social Life of the Chinese*, "though all deprecate it as contrary to the dictates of reason and the instincts of nature, many are ready boldly to apologize for it and declare it to be necessary, especially in the families of the excessively poor."

Here again the wide prevalence of the custom. is the first and best proof that women are driven by some great pressure within themselves to accede to it. If further proof were necessary, it is afforded by the testimony of Occidentals who have lived in China, that Chinese midwives are extremely skillful in producing early abortion. Abortions are not performed without the consent and usually only at the demand of the woman.

In China, as in India, the religions of the country condemned, even as they to-day condemn, infanticide. Both foreign and native governments have sought to make an end of the custom. But in both countries it still prevails. Nor are these Eastern countries substantially different from their Western neighbors.

The record of Western Europe is summarized by Oscar Helmuth Werner, Ph.D., in his book, *The Unmarried Mother in German Literature*." "Infanticide," says Dr. Werner, "was the most common crime in Western Europe from the Middle Ages down to the end of the Eighteenth Century." This fact, of course, means that it was even more largely practiced by the married than the unmarried, the married mothers being far greater in number.

"Another problem which confronted the church," he says in another place, "was the practice of exposure and killing of children by legal parents." A sort of final word from Dr. Werner is this: "Infanticide by legal parents has practically ceased in civilized countries, but abortion, its substitute, has not."

How desperately woman desired freedom to develop herself as an individual, apart from motherhood, is indicated by the fact that infanticide was "the most common crime of Western Europe," in spite of the fact that some of the most terrible punishments ever inflicted by law were meted out to those women who sought this means of escape from the burden of unwanted children. Dr. Werner shows that in Germany, for instance, in the year 1532, it was the law that those guilty of infanticide were "to be buried alive or impaled. In order to prevent desperation, however, they shall be drowned if it is possible to get to a stream or river, in which they shall be torn with glowing tongs beforehand."

Notwithstanding the fact that at one time in Germany, the punishment was that of drowning in a sack containing a serpent, a cat and a dog--in order that the utmost agony might be inflicted--one sovereign alone condemned 20,000 women to death for infanticide, without noticeably reducing the practice.

To-day, in spite of the huge numbers of abortions and the multiplication of foundlings' homes and orphans' asylums, infanticide is still an occasional crime in all countries. As to woman's share in the practice, let us add this word from Havelock Ellis, taken from the chapter on "Morbid Psychic Phenomena" in his book, *Man and Woman*:

"Infanticide is the crime in which women stand out in the greatest contrast to men; in Italy, for example, for every 100 men guilty of infanticide, there are 477 women." And he remarks later that when a man commits this crime, "he usually does it at the instance of some woman."

Infanticide tends to disappear as skill in producing abortions is developed or knowledge of contraceptives is spread, and only then. One authority, as will be seen in a later chapter, estimates the number of abortions performed annually in the United States at 1,000,000, and another believes that double that number are produced.

"Among the Hindus and Mohammedans, artificial abortion is extremely common," says Westermark. "In Persia every illegitimate pregnancy ends with abortion. In Turkey, both among the rich and the poor, even married women very commonly procure abortion after they have given birth to two children, one of which is a boy."

The nations mentioned are typical of the world, except those countries where information concerning contraceptives has enabled women to limit their families without recourse to operations.

It is apparent that nothing short of contraceptives can put an end to the horrors of abortion and infanticide. The Roman Catholic church, which has fought these practices from the beginning, has been unable to check them; and no more powerful agency could have been brought into play. It took that church, even in the days of its unlimited power, many centuries to come to its present sweeping condemnation of abortion. The severity of the condemnation depended upon the time at which the development of the fœtus was interfered with. An illuminating resume of the church's efforts in this direction is given by Dr. William Burke Ryan in his authoritative and exhaustive study entitled "*Infanticide; Its Law, Prevalence, Prevention and History.*" Dr. Ryan says: "Theologians of the church of Rome made a distinction between the inanimate and the animate fœtus to which the soul is added by the creation of God, and adopted the opinions of some of the old philosophers, more particularly those of Aristotle, as to animation in the male and female, but the canon law altogether negative the doctrine of the Stoics, for Innocent II condemned the following proposition:

"'It seems probable that the fœtus does not possess a rational soul as long as it is in the womb, and only begins to possess it when born, and consequently in no abortion is homicide committed.' Sextus V inflicted severe penalties for the crime of abortion at any period; these were in some degree mitigated by Gregory XIV, who, however, still held that those producing the abortion of an animated fœtus should be subject to them, viz., and excommunication reserved to the bishop and also an 'irregularity' reserved to the Pope himself for absolution."

To-day, the Roman church stands firmly upon the proposition that "directly intended, artificial abortion must be regarded as wrongful killing, as murder."[*] But it required a long time for it to reach that point, in the face of the demand for relief from large families.

[* Pastoral Medicine.]

As it was with the fight of the church against abortion, so it is with the effort to prevent abortion in the United States to-day. All efforts to stop the practice are futile. Apparently, the numbers of these illegal operations are increasing from year to year. From year to year more women will undergo the humiliation, the danger and the horror of them, and the terrible record, begun with the infanticide of the primitive peoples, will go on piling up its volume of human misery and racial damage, until society awakens to the fact that a fundamental remedy must be applied.

To apply such a remedy, society must recognize the terrible lesson taught by the innumerable centuries of infanticide and fœticide. If these abhorrent practices could have been ended by punishment and suppression, they would have ceased long ago. But to continue suppression and punishment, and let the matter rest there, is only to miss the lesson--only to permit conditions to go from bad to worse.

What is that lesson? It is this: woman's desire for freedom is born of the feminine spirit, which is the absolute, elemental, inner urge of womanhood. It is the strongest force in her nature; it cannot be destroyed; it can merely be diverted from its natural expression into violent and destructive channels.

The chief obstacles to the normal expression of this force are undesired pregnancy and the burden of unwanted children. These obstacles have always been and always will be swept aside by a considerable proportion of women. Driven by the irresistible force within them, they will always seek wider freedom and greater self-development, regardless of the cost. The sole question that society has to answer is, how shall women be permitted to attain this end?

Are you horrified at the record set down in this chapter? It is well that you should be. You cannot help society to apply the fundamental remedy unless you know these facts and are conscious of their fullest significance. Society, in dealing with the feminine spirit, has its choice of clearly defined alternatives. It can continue to resort to violence in an effort to enslave the elemental urge of womanhood, making of woman a mere instrument of reproduction and punishing her when she revolts. Or, it can permit her to choose whether she shall become a mother and how many children she will have. It can go on trying to crush that which is un crushable, or it can recognize woman's claim to freedom, and cease to impose diverting and destructive barriers. If we choose the latter course, we must not only remove all restrictions upon the use of scientific contraceptives, but we must legalize and encourage their use.

This problem comes home with peculiar force to the people of America. Do we want the millions of abortions performed annually to be multiplied? Do we want the precious, tender qualities of womanhood, so much needed for our racial development, to perish in these sordid, abnormal experiences? Or, do we wish to permit woman to find her way to fundamental freedom through safe, unobjectionable, scientific means? We have our choice. Upon our answer to these questions depends in a tremendous degree the character and the capabilities of the future American race.

CHAPTER III

THE MATERIALS OF THE NEW RACE

EACH of us has an ideal of what the American of the future should be. We have been told times without number that out of the mixture of stocks, the intermingling of ideas and aspirations, there is to come a race greater than any which has contributed to the population of the United States. What is the basis for this hope that is so generally indulged in? If the hope is founded upon realities, how may it be realized? To understand the difficulties and the obstacles to be overcome before the dream of a greater race in America can be attained, is to understand something of the task before the women who shall give birth to that race.

What material is there for a greater American race? What elements make up our present millions? Where do they live? How do they live? In what direction does our national civilization bend their ideals?

What is the effect of the "melting pot" upon the foreigner, once he begins to "melt"? Are we now producing a freer, juster, more intelligent, more idealistic, creative people out of the varied ingredients here?

Before we can answer these questions, we must consider briefly the races which have contributed to American population.

Among our more than 100,000,000 population are Negroes, Indians, Chinese and other colored people to the number of 11,000,000. There are also 14,500,000 persons of foreign birth. Besides these there are 14,000,000 children of foreign-born parents and 6,500,000 persons whose fathers or mothers were born on foreign soil, making a total of 46,000,000 people of foreign stock. Fifty per cent of our population is of the native white strain.

Of the foreign stock in the United States, the last general census, compiled in 1910, shows that 25.7 per cent was German, 14 per cent was Irish, 8.5 per cent was Russian or Finnish, 7.2 was English, 6.5 per cent Italian and 6.2 per cent Austrian. The Abstract of the same census points out several significant facts. The Western European strains in this country are represented by a majority of native-born children of foreign-born or mixed parentage. This is because the immigration from those sources has been checked. On the other hand, immigration from Southern and Eastern Europe, including Russia and Finland, increased 175.4 per cent from 1900 to 1910. During that period, the slums of Europe dumped their submerged inhabitants into America at a rate almost double that of the preceding decade, and the flow was still increasing at the time the census was taken. So it is more than likely that when the next census is taken it will be found that following 1910 there was an even greater flow from Spain, Italy, Hungary, Austria, Russia, Finland, and other countries where the iron hand of economic and political tyrannies 'had crushed great populations into ignorance and want. These peoples have not been in the United States long enough to produce great families. The census of 1920 will in all probability tell a story of a greater and more serious problem than did the last.

Over one-fourth of all the immigrants over fourteen years of age, admitted during the two decades preceding 1910, were illiterate. Of the 8,398,000 who arrived in the 1900-1910 period, 2,238,000 could not read or write. There were 1,600,000 illiterate foreigners in the United States when the 1910 census was taken. Do these elements give promise of a better race? Are we doing anything genuinely constructive to overcome this situation?

Two-thirds of the white foreign stock in the United States live in cities. Four-fifths of the populations of Chicago and New York are of this stock. More than two-thirds of the populations of Boston, Cleveland, Detroit, Buffalo, Pittsburgh, Milwaukee, Newark, Jersey City, Providence, Worcester, Scranton, Paterson, Fall River, Lowell, Cambridge, Bridgeport, St. Paul, Minneapolis and San Francisco are of other than native white ancestry. Of the fifty principal cities of the United States there are only fourteen in which fifty per cent of the population is of unmixed native white parentage.

Only one state in the Union--North Carolina--has less than one per cent of the white foreign stock. New York, New Jersey, Delaware, Massachusetts, Connecticut, Rhode Island, Michigan, Illinois, Wisconsin, Minnesota, the Dakotas, Montana and Utah have more than fifty per cent foreign stock. Eleven states, including those on the Pacific Coast, have from 35 to 50 per cent. Maine, Ohio and Kansas have from 25 to 35 per cent. Maryland, Indiana, Missouri and Texas have from 15 to 25 per cent. These proportions are increasing rather than decreasing, owing to the extraordinarily high birth rate of the foreign strains.

A special analysis of 1915 vital statistics for certain states, in the World Almanac for 1918, shows that foreign-born mothers gave birth to nearly 62 per cent of the children born in Connecticut, nearly 58 per cent in Massachusetts, nearly 33 per cent in Michigan, nearly 58 per cent in Rhode Island, more than 43 per cent in New Hampshire, more than 54 per cent in New York and more than 38 per cent in Pennsylvania.

All these figures, be it remembered, fail to include foreign stock of the second generation after landing. If the statistics for children who have native parents but foreign-born grandparents, or who have one foreign-born parent, were given, they would doubtless leave but a small percentage of births from stocks native to the soil for several generations.

Immigrants or their children constitute the majority of workers employed in many of our industries. "Seven out of ten of those who work in our iron and steel industries are drawn from this class," says the National Geographic Magazine (February, 1917), "seven out of ten of our bituminous coal miners belong to it. Three out of four who work in packing towns were born abroad or are children of those who were born abroad; four out of five of those who make our silk goods, seven out of eight of those employed in woolen mills, nine out of ten of those who refine our petroleum, and nineteen out of twenty of those who manufacture our sugar are immigrants or the children of immigrants." And it might have shown a similarly high percentage of those in the ready-made clothing industries, railway and public works construction of the less skilled sort, and a number of others.

That these foreigners who have come in hordes have brought with them their ignorance of hygiene and modern ways of living and that they are handicapped by religious superstitions is only too true. But they also bring in their hearts a desire for freedom from all the tyrannies that afflict the earth. They would not be here if they did not bear within them the hardihood of pioneers, a courage of no mean order. They have the simple faith that in America they will find equality, liberty and an opportunity for a decent livelihood. And they have something else. The cell plasms of these peoples are freighted with the potentialities of the best in Old World civilization., They come from lands rich in the traditions of courage, of art, music, letters, science and philosophy. Americans no longer consider themselves cultured unless they have journeyed to these lands to find access to the treasures created by men and women of this same blood. The immigrant brings the possibilities of all these things to our shores, but where is the opportunity to reproduce in the New World the cultures of the old?

What opportunities have we given to these peoples to enrich our civilization? We have greeted them as "a lot of ignorant foreigners," we have shouted at, bustled and kicked them. Our industries have taken advantage of their ignorance of the country's ways to take their toil in mills and mines and factories at starvation wages. We have herded them into slums to become diseased, to become social burdens or to die. We have huddled them together like rabbits to multiply their numbers and their misery. Instead of saying that we Americanize them, we should confess that we animalize them. The only freedom we seem to have given them is the freedom to make heavier and more secure their chains. What hope is there for racial progress in this human material, treated more carelessly and brutally than the cheapest factory product?

Nor are all our social handicaps bound up in the immigrant. There were in the United States, when the Federal Industrial Relations Committee finished its work in 1915, several million migratory workers, most of them white, many of them married but separated from their families, who were compelled, like themselves, to struggle with dire want.

There were in 1910 more than 2,353,000 tenant farmers, two-thirds of whom lived and worked under the terrible conditions which the Industrial Relations Commission's report showed to prevail in the South and Southwest. These tenant farmers, as the report showed, were always in want, and were compelled by the very terms of the prevailing tenant contracts to produce children who must go to the fields and do the work of adults. The census proved that this tenancy was on the increase, the number of tenants in all but the New England and Middle Atlantic States having increased approximately 30 per cent from 1900 to 1910.

Moreover, there were in the United States in 1910 5,516,163 illiterates. Of these 1,378,884 were of pure native white stock. In some states in the South as much as 29 per cent of the population is illiterate, many of these, of course, being Negroes.

There is still another factor to be considered--a factor which because of its great scope is more ominous than any yet mentioned. This is the underpaid mass of workers in the United States-- workers whose low wages are forcing them deeper into want each day. Let Senator Borah, not a radical nor even a reformer, but a leader of the Republican party, tell the story. "Fifty-seven per cent of the families in the United States have incomes of $800 or less," said he in a speech before the Senate, August 24, 1917, "Seventy per cent of the families of our country have incomes of $1,000 or less. Tell me how a man so situated can have shelter for his family; how he can provide food and clothing. He is an industrial peon. His home is scant and pinched beyond the power of language to tell. He sees his wife and children on the ragged edge of hunger from week to week and month to month. If sickness comes, he faces suicide or crime. He cannot educate his children; he cannot fit them for citizenship; he cannot even fit them as soldiers to die for their country.

"It is the tragedy of our whole national life--how these people live in such times as these. We have not yet gathered the fruits of such an industrial condition in this country. We have been saved thus far by reason of the newness of our national life, our vast public lands now almost exhausted, our great natural resources now fast being seized and held, but the hour of reckoning will come."

Senator Borah was thinking, doubtless, of open revolution, of bloodshed and the destruction of property. In a far more terrible sense, the reckoning which he has referred to is already upon us. The ills we suffer as the result of the conditions now prevailing in the United States are appalling in their sum.

It is these conditions that produce the 3,000,000 child laborers of the United States; child slaves who undergo hardships that blight them physically and mentally, leaving them fit only to produce human beings whose deficiencies arid misfortunes will exceed their own.

From these same elements, living under these same conditions come the feebleminded and other defectives. Just how many feebleminded there are in the United States, no one knows, because no attempt has ever been made to give public care to all of them, and families are more inclined to conceal than to reveal the mental defects of their members. Estimates vary from 350,000 at the present time to nearly 400,000 as early as 1890, Henry H. Goddard, Ph. D., of the Vineland, N. J., Training School, being authority for the latter statement. Only 34,137 of these unfortunates were under institutional care in the United States in 1916, the rest being free to propagate their kind--piling up public burdens for future generations. The feebleminded are notoriously prolific in reproduction. The close relationship between poverty and ignorance and the production of feebleminded is shown by Anne Moore, Ph. D., in a report to the Public Education Association of New York in 1911. She found that an overwhelming proportion of the classified feebleminded children in New York schools came from large families living in overcrowded slum conditions, and that only a small percentage were born of native parents.

Sixty thousand prostitutes go and come anew each year in the United States. This army of unfortunates, as social workers and scientists testify, come from families living under like conditions of want.

In the New York City schools alone in December, 1916, 61 per cent of the children were suffering from undernourishment and 21 per cent in immediate danger of it. These facts, also the result of the conditions outlined, were discovered by the city Bureau of Child Hygiene.

Another item in the sordid list is that of venereal disease. In his pamphlet entitled "*The Venereal Diseases*," issued in 1918, Dr. Hermann M. Biggs head of the New York State Department of Health quoted authorities who gave estimates of the amount of syphilis and gonorrhea in the United States. One says that 60 per cent of the men contract one disease or the other at some time. Another said that 40 per cent of the population of New York City had syphilis, one of the most terrible of all maladies. Poverty, delayed marriage, prostitution--a brief and terrible chain accounts for this scourge.

Finally, there is tuberculosis, bred by bad housing conditions and contributed to in frightful measure by poor food and unhealthy surroundings during the hours of employment. Dr. Frederick L. Hoffman, director of the National Association for the Study and Prevention of

Tuberculosis and foremost statistical authority upon tuberculosis in the United States, says: "We know of 2,000,000 tubercular persons in the United States."

Does this picture horrify the reader? This is not the whole truth. A few scattered statistics lack the power to reflect the broken lives of overworked fathers, the ceaseless, increasing pain of overburdened mothers and the agony of childhood fighting its way against the handicaps of ill health, insufficient food, inadequate training and stifling toil.

Can we expect to remedy this situation by dismissing the problem of the submerged native elements with legislative palliatives or treating it with careless scorn? Do we better it by driving out of the immigrant's heart the dream of liberty that brought him to our shores? Do we solve the problem by giving him, instead of an opportunity to develop his own culture, low wages, a home in the slums and those pseudo-patriotic preachments which constitute our machine-made "Americanization"?

Every detail of this sordid situation means a problem that must be solved before we can even clear the way for a greater race in America. Nor is there any hope of solving any of these problems if we continue to attack them in the usual way.

Men have sentimentalized about them and legislated upon them. They have denounced them and they have applied reforms. But it has all been ridiculously, cruelly futile.

This is the condition of things for which those stand who demand more and more children. Each child born under such conditions but makes them worse--each child in its own person suffers the consequence of the intensified evils.

If we are to develop in America a new race with a racial soul, we must keep the birth rate within the scope of our ability to understand as well as to educate. We must not encourage reproduction beyond our capacity to assimilate our numbers so as to make the coming generation into such physically fit, mentally capable, socially alert individuals as are the ideal of a democracy.

The intelligence of a people is of slow evolutional development--it lags far behind the reproductive ability. It is far too slow to cope with conditions created by an increasing population, unless that increase is carefully regulated.

We must, therefore, not permit an increase in population that we are not prepared to care for to the best advantage--that we are not prepared to do justice to, educationally and economically. We must popularize birth control thinking. We must not leave it haphazardly to be the privilege of the already privileged. We must put this means of freedom and growth into the bands of the masses.

We must set motherhood free. We must give the foreign and submerged mother knowledge that will enable her to prevent bringing to birth children she does not want. We know that in each of these submerged and semi submerged elements of the population there are rich factors of racial culture. Motherhood is the channel through which these cultures flow. Motherhood, when free to choose the father, free to choose the time and the number of children who shall result from the union, automatically works in wondrous ways. It refuses to bring forth weaklings; refuses to bring forth slaves; refuses to bear children who must live under the conditions described. It withholds the unfit, brings forth the fit; brings few children into homes where there is not sufficient to provide for them. Instinctively it avoids all those things which multiply racial handicaps. Under such circumstances we can hope that the "melting pot" will refine. We shall see that it will save the precious metals of racial culture, fused into an amalgam of physical perfection, mental strength and spiritual progress. Such an American race, containing the best of all racial elements, could give to the world a vision and a leadership beyond our present imagination.

CHAPTER IV

TWO CLASSES OF WOMEN

THUS far we have been discussing mainly one class in America--the workers. Most women who belong to the workers' families have no accurate or reliable knowledge of contraceptives, and are, therefore, bringing children into the world so rapidly that they, their families and their class are overwhelmed with numbers. Out of these numbers, as has been shown, have grown many of the burdens with which society in general is weighted; out of them have come, also, the want, disease, hard living conditions and general misery of the workers.

The women of this class are the greatest sufferers of all. Not only do they bear the material hardships and deprivations in common with the rest of the family, but in the case of the mother, these are intensified. It is the man and the child who have first call upon the insufficient amount of food. It is the man and the child who get the recreation, if there is any to be had, for the man's hours of labor are usually limited by law or by his labor union.

It is the woman who suffers first from hunger, the woman whose clothing is least adequate, the woman who must work all hours, even though she is not compelled, as in the case of millions, to go into a factory to add to her husband's scanty income. It is she, too, whose health breaks first and most hopelessly, under the long hours of work, the drain of frequent childbearing, and often almost constant nursing of babies. There are no eight-hour laws to protect the mother against overwork and toil in the home; no laws to protect her against ill health and the diseases of pregnancy and reproduction. In fact there has been almost no thought or consideration given for the protection of the mother in the home of the workingman.

There are no general health statistics to tell the full story of the physical ills suffered by women as a result of too great reproductivity. But we get some light upon conditions through the statistics on maternal mortality, compiled by Dr. Grace L. Meigs, for the Children's Bureau of the United States Department of Labor. These figures do not include the deaths of women suffering from diseases complicated by pregnancy.

"In 1913, in this country at least 15,000 women, it is estimated, died from conditions caused by childbirth; about 7,000 of these died from childbed fever and the remaining 8,000 from diseases now known to be to a great extent preventable or curable," says Dr. Meigs in her summary, "Physicians and statisticians agree that these figures are a *great underestimate*."

Think of it--the needless deaths of 15,000 women a "great underestimate"! Yet even this number means that virtually every hour of the day and night two women die as the result of childbirth in the healthiest and supposedly the most progressive country in the world.

It is apparent that Dr. Meigs leaves out of consideration the many thousands of deaths each year of women who become pregnant while suffering from tuberculosis. Dr. S. Adolphus Knopf, addressing the forty-fourth annual convention of the American Public

Health Association, in Cincinnati in 1916, called attention to the fact that some authors hold that "65 per cent of the Women afflicted with tuberculosis, even when afflicted only in the relatively early and curable stages, die as the result of pregnancy which could have been avoided and their lives saved had they but known some means of prevention." Nor were syphilis, various kidney and heart disorders and other diseases, often rendered fatal by pregnancy, taken into account by Dr. Meigs' survey.

Still, leaving out all the hundreds of thousands of women who die because pregnancy has complicated serious diseases, Dr. Meigs finds that "in 1913, the death rate per 100,000 of the population from all conditions caused by childbirth was little lower than that from typhoid fever. This rate would be almost quadrupled if only the group of the population which can be affected, women of childbearing ages, were considered. In 1913, childbirth caused more deaths among women 15 to 44 years old than any disease except tuberculosis."

From what sort of homes come these deaths from childbirth? Most of them occur in overcrowded dwellings, where food, care, sanitation, nursing and medical attention are inadequate. Where do we find most of the tuberculosis and much of the other disease which is aggravated by pregnancy? In the same sort of home.

The deadly chain of misery is all too plain to anyone who takes the trouble to observe it. A woman of the working class marries and with her husband lives in a degree of comfort upon his earnings. Her household duties are not beyond her strength. Then the children begin to come-- one, two, three, four, possibly five or more. The earnings of the husband do not increase as rapidly as the family does. Food, clothing and general comfort in the home grow less as the numbers of the family increase. The woman's work grows heavier, and her strength is less with each child. Possibly--probably--she has to go into a factory to add to her husband's earnings. There she toils, doing her housework at night. Her health goes, and the crowded conditions and lack of necessities in the home help to bring about disease--especially tuberculosis. {p. 52}
Under the circumstances, the woman's chances of recovering from each succeeding childbirth grow less. Less too are the chances of the child's surviving, as shown by tables in another chapter. Unwanted children, poverty, ill health, misery, death-these are the links in the chain, and they are common to most of the families in the class described in the preceding chapter.

Nor is the full story of the woman's sufferings yet told. Grievous as is her material condition, her spiritual deprivations are still greater. By the very fact of its existence, mother love demands its expression toward the child. By that same fact, it becomes a necessary factor in the child's development. The mother of too many children, in a crowded home where want, ill health and antagonism are perpetually created, is deprived of this simplest personal expression. She can give nothing to her child of herself, of her personality. Training is impossible and sympathetic guidance equally so. Instead, such a mother is tired, nervous, irritated and ill-tempered; a determent, often, instead of a help to her children. Motherhood becomes a disaster and childhood a tragedy.

It goes without saying that this woman loses also all opportunity of personal expression outside her home. She has neither a chance to develop social qualities nor to indulge in social pleasures. The feminine element in her--that spirit which blossoms forth now and then in women free from such burdens--cannot assert itself. She can contribute nothing to the wellbeing of the community. She is a breeding machine and a drudge--she is not an asset but a liability to her neighborhood, to her class, to society. She can be nothing as long as she is denied means of limiting her family.

In sharp contrast with these women who ignorantly bring forth large families and who thereby enslave themselves, we find a few women who have one, two or three children or no children at all. These women, with the exception of the childless ones, live full-rounded lives. They are found not only in the ranks of the rich and the well-to-do, but in the ranks of labor as well. They have but one point of basic difference from their enslaved sisters--they are not burdened with the rearing of large families.

We have no need to call upon the historian, the sociologist nor the statistician for our knowledge of this situation. We meet it every day in the ordinary routine of our lives. The women who are the great teachers, the great writers, the artists, musicians, physicians, the leaders of public movements, the great suffragists, reformers, labor leaders and revolutionaries are those who are not compelled to give lavishly of their physical and spiritual strength in bearing and rearing large families. The situation is too familiar for discussion. Where a woman with a large family is contributing directly to the progress of her times or the betterment of social conditions, it is usually because she has sufficient wealth to employ trained nurses, governesses, and others who perform the duties necessary to child rearing. She is a rarity and is universally recognized as such.

The women with small families, however, are free to make their choice of those social pleasures which are the right of every human being and necessary to each one's full development. {p. 55} They can be and are, each according to her individual capacity, comrades and companions to their husbands--a privilege denied to the mother of many children. Theirs is the opportunity to keep abreast of the times, to make and cultivate a varied circle of friends, to seek amusements as suits their taste and means, to know the meaning of real recreation. All these things remain unrealized desires to the prolific mother.

Women who have a knowledge of contraceptives are not compelled to make the choice between a maternal experience and a marred love life; they are not forced to balance motherhood against social and spiritual activities. Motherhood is for them to choose, as it should be for every woman to choose. Choosing to become mothers, they do not thereby shut themselves away from thorough companionship with their husbands, from friends, from culture, from all those manifold experiences which are necessary to the completeness and the joy of life.

Fit mothers of the race are these, the courted comrades of the men they choose, rather than the "slaves of slaves." For theirs is the magic power--the power of limiting their families to such numbers as will permit them to live full-rounded lives. Such lives are the expression of the feminine spirit which is woman *and all of her*--not merely art, nor professional skill, nor intellect--but all that woman is, or may achieve.

CHAPTER V

THE WICKEDNESS OF CREATING LARGE FAMILIES

THE most serious evil of our times is that of encouraging the bringing into the world of large families. The most immoral practice of the day is breeding too many children. These statements may startle those who have never made a thorough investigation of the problem. They are, nevertheless, well considered, and the truth of them is abundantly borne out by an examination of facts and conditions which are part of everyday experience or observation.

The immorality of large families lies not only in their injury to the members of those families but in their injury to society. If one were asked offhand to name the greatest evil of the day one might, in the light of one's education by the newspapers, or by agitators, make any one of a number of replies. One might say prostitution, the oppression of labor, child labor, or war. Yet the poverty and neglect which drives a girl into prostitution usually has its source in a family too large to be properly cared for by the mother, if the girl is not actually subnormal because her mother bore too many children, and, therefore, the more likely to become a prostitute. Labor is oppressed because it is too plentiful; wages go up and conditions improve when labor is scarce. Large families make plentiful labor and they also provide the workers for the child-labor factories as well as the armies of unemployed. That population, swelled by over breeding, is a classic cause of war, we shall see in a later chapter. Without the large family, not one of these evils could exist to any considerable extent, much less to the extent that they exist to-day. The large family--especially the family too large to receive adequate care--is the one thing necessary to the perpetuation of these and other evils and is therefore a greater evil than any one of them.

First of the manifold immoralities involved in the producing of a large family is the outrage upon the womanhood of the mother. If no mother bore children against her will or against her feminine instinct, there would be few large families. The average mother of a baby every year or two has been forced into unwilling motherhood, so far as the later arrivals are concerned. It is not the less immoral when the power which compels enslavement is the church, state or the propaganda of well-meaning patriots clamoring against "race suicide." The wrong is as great as if the enslaving force were the unbridled passions of her husband. The wrong to the unwilling mother, deprived of her liberty, and all opportunity of self-development, is in itself enough to condemn large families as immoral.

The outrage upon the woman does not end there, however. Excessive childbearing is now recognized by the medical profession as one of the most prolific causes of ill health in women. There are in America hundreds of thousands of women, in good health when they married, who have within a few years become physical wrecks, incapable of mothering their children, incapable of enjoying life.

"Every physician," writes Dr. Wm. J. Robinson in *Birth Control or The Limitation of Offspring*," knows that too frequent childbirth, nursing and the sleepless nights that are required in bringing up a child exhaust the vitality of thousands of mothers, make them prematurely old, or turn them into chronic invalids."

The effect of the large family upon the father is only less disastrous than it is upon the mother. The spectacle of the young man, happy in health, strength and the prospect of a joyful love life, makes us smile in sympathy. But this same young man ten years later is likely to present a spectacle as sorry as it is familiar. If he finds that the children come one after another at short intervals-so fast indeed that no matter how hard he works, nor how many hours, he cannot keep pace with their needs -the lover whom all the world loves will have been converted into a disheartened, threadbare incompetent, whom all the world pities or despises. Instead of being the happy, competent father, supporting one or two children as they should be supported, he is the frantic struggler against the burden of five or six, with the tragic prospect of several more. The ranks of the physically weakened, mentally dejected and spiritually hopeless young fathers of large families attest all too strongly the immorality of the system.

If its effects upon the mother and the wage-earning father were not enough to condemn the large family as an institution, its effects upon the child would make the case against it conclusive. In the United States, some 300,000 children under one year of age die each twelve months. Approximately ninety per cent of these deaths are directly or indirectly due to malnutrition, to other diseased conditions resulting from poverty, or, to excessive childbearing by the mother.

The direct relationship between the size of the wage-earner's family and the death of children less than one year old has been revealed by a number of studies of the infant death-rate. One of the clearest of these was that made by Arthur Geissler among miners and cited by Dr. Alfred Ploetz before the First International Eugenic Congress.[*] Taking 26,000 births from unselected marriages, and omitting families having one and two children, Geissler got this result:

Deaths During First Year.

1st born children	23%
2nd	20%
3rd	21%
4th	23%
5th	26%

6th	29%
7th	31%
8th	33%
9th	36%
10th	41%
11th	51%
12th	60%

Thus we see that the second and third children have a very good chance to live through the first year. Children arriving later have less and less chance, until the twelfth has hardly any chance at all to live twelve months. This does not complete the case, however, for those who care to go farther into the subject will find that many of those who live for a year die before they reach the age of five. Many, perhaps, will think it idle to go farther in demonstrating the immorality of large families, but since there is still an abundance of proof at hand, it may be offered for the, sake of those who find difficulty in adjusting old-fashioned ideas to the facts. The most merciful thing that the large family does to one of its infant members is to kill it. The same factors which create the terrible infant mortality rate, and which swell the death rate of children between the ages of one and five, operate even more extensively to lower the health rate of the surviving members. Moreover, the overcrowded homes of large families reared in poverty further contribute to this condition. Lack of medical attention is still another factor, so that the child who must struggle for health in competition with other members of a closely packed family has still great difficulties to meet after its poor constitution and malnutrition have been accounted for.

The probability of a child handicapped by a weak constitution, an overcrowded home, inadequate food and care, and possibly a deficient mental equipment, winding up in prison or an almshouse, is too evident for comment. Every jail, hospital for the insane, reformatory and institution for the feebleminded cries out against the evils of too prolific breeding among wage-workers.

We shall see when we come to consider the relation of voluntary motherhood to the rights of labor and to the prevention of war that the large family of the worker makes possible his oppression, and that it also is the chief cause of such human holocausts as the one just closed after the four and a half bloodiest years in history. No such extended consideration is necessary to indicate from what source the young slaves in the child-labor factories come. They come from large impoverished families--from families in which the older children must put their often feeble strength to the task of supporting the younger.

The immorality of bringing large families into the world is recognized by those who are combatting the child-labor evil. Mary Alden Hopkins, writing in Harper's Weekly in 1915, quotes Owen R. Lovejoy, general secretary of the National Child Labor-Committee, as follows:

"How many are too many? . . . Any more than the mother can look after and the father make a living for . . . Under present conditions as soon as there are too many children for the father to feed, some of them go to work in the mine or factory or store or mill near by. In doing this, they not only injure their tender growing bodies, but indirectly, they drag down the father's wage . . .The home becomes a mere rendezvous for the nightly gathering of bodies numb with weariness and minds drunk with sleep." And if they survive the factory, they marry to perpetuate and multiply their ignorance, weakness and diseases.

What have large families to do with prostitution? Ask anyone who has studied the problem. The size of the family has a direct bearing on the lives of thousands of girls who are living in prostitution. Poverty, lack of care and training during adolescence, overcrowded housing conditions which accompany large families are universally recognized causes of "waywardness" in girls. Social workers have cried out in vain against these conditions, pointing to their inevitable results.

In the foreword to "Downward Paths," A. Maude Royden says: "Intimately connected with this aspect of the question is that of home and housing, especially of the child. The age at which children are first corrupted is almost incredibly early, until we consider the nature of the surroundings in which they grow up. Insufficient space, over-crowding, the herding together of all ages and both sexes--these things break down the barriers of a natural modesty and reserve. Where decency is practically impossible, unchastity will follow, and follow almost as a matter of course." And the child who has no place to play except in the street, who lacks mother care, whose chief emotional experience is the longing for the necessities of life? We know too well the end of the sorry tale. The forlorn figures of the shadows where lurk the girls who sell themselves that they may eat and be clothed rise up to damn the moral dogmatists, who mouth their sickening exhortations to the wives and mothers of the workers to breed, breed, breed.

The evidence is conclusive as regards the large family of the wage-worker. Social workers, physicians and reformers cry out to stop the breeding of these, who must exist in want until they become permanent members of the ranks of the unfit. But what of the family of the wealthy or the merely well-to-do? It is among these classes that we find the women who have attained to voluntary motherhood. It is to these classes, too, that the "race suicide" alarmists have from time to time addressed specially emphasized pleas for more children. The advocates of more prolific breeding urge that these same women have more intelligence, better health, more time to care for children and more means to support them. They therefore declare that it is the duty of such women to populate the land with strong, healthy, intelligent offspring--to bear children in great numbers.

It is high time to expose the sheer foolishness of this argument. The first absurdity is that the women who are in comfortable circumstances could continue to be cultured and of social value if they were the mothers of large families. Neither could they maintain their present standard of health nor impart it to their children.

While it is true that they have resources at their command which case the burden of childbearing and child rearing immeasurably, it is also true that the wealthy mother, as well as the poverty-stricken mother, must give from her own system certain elements which it takes time to replace. Excessive childbearing is harder on the woman who lacks care than on the one who does not, but both alike must give their bodies time to recover from the strain of childbearing. If the women in fortunate circumstances gave ear to the demand of masculine "race-suicide"[*] {*there is no footnote on this page; the footnote this refers to is at the end of the chapter on page 71--jbh*} fanatics they could within a few years be down to the condition of their sisters who lack time to cultivate their talents and intellects. A vigorous, intelligent, fruitfully cultured motherhood is all but impossible if no restriction is placed by that motherhood upon the number of children.

Wage-workers and salaried people have a vital interest in the size of the families of those better situated in life. Large families among the rich are immoral not only because they invade the natural right of woman to the control of her own body, to self-development and to self-expression, but because they are oppressive to the poorer elements of society. If the upper and middle classes of society had kept pace with the poorer elements of society in reproduction during the past fifty years, the working class to-day would be forced down to the level of the Chinese whose wage standard is said to be a few handfuls of rice a day.

If these considerations are not enough to halt the masculine advocate of large families who reminds us of the days of our mothers and grandmothers, let it be remembered that bearing and rearing six or eight children to-day is a far different matter from what it was in the generations just preceding. Physically and nervously, the woman of to-day is not fitted to bear children as frequently as was her mother and her mother's mother. The high tension of .modern life and the complicating of woman's everyday existence have doubtless contributed to this result. And who of us can say, until a careful scientific investigation is made, how much the rapid development of tuberculosis and other grave diseases, even among the well-nurtured, may be due to the depletion of the physical capital of the unborn by the too prolific childbearing of preceding generations of mothers?

The immorality of bringing into being a large family is a wrong-doing shared by three--the mother, the father and society. Upon all three falls the burden of guilt. It may be said for the mother and father that they are usually ignorant. What shall be said of society? What shall be said of us who permit outworn laws and customs to persist in piling up the appalling sum of public expense, misery and spiritual degradation? The indictment against the large unwanted family is written in human woe. Who in the light of intelligent understanding shall have the brazenness to stand up and defend it?

One thing we know--the woman who has escaped the chains of too great reproductivity will never again wear them. The birth rate of the wealthy and upper classes will never appreciably rise. The woman of these classes is free of her most oppressive bonds. Being free, we have a right to expect much of her. We expect her to give still greater expression to her feminine spirit--we expect her to enrich the intellectual, artistic, moral and spiritual life of the world.

We expect her to demolish old systems of morals, a degenerate prudery, Dark-Age religious concepts, laws that enslave women by denying them the knowledge of their bodies, and information as to contraceptives. These must go to the scrapheap of vicious, cast-off things. Hers is the power to send them there. Shall we look to her to strike the first blow which shall wrench her sisters from the grip of the dead hand of the past?

[* Interesting and perhaps surprising light is thrown upon the origin of the term "race suicide" by the following quotation from an article by Harold Bolce in the Cosmopolitan (New York) for May, 1909:

"'The sole effect of prolificacy is to fill the cemeteries with tiny graves, sacrifices of the innocents to the Moloch of immoderate maternity.' Thus insists Edward A. Ross, Professor of Sociology in the University of Wisconsin; and he protests against the 'dwarfing of women and the cheapening of men' as regards the restriction of the birth rate as a 'movement at bottom salutary, and its evils minor, transient and curable.' This is virile gospel, and particularly significant coming from the teacher who invented the term 'race suicide,' which many have erroneously attributed to Mr. Roosevelt."]

CHAPTER VI

CRIES OF DESPAIR AND SOCIETY'S PROBLEMS

BEFORE we pass to a further consideration of our subject, shall we not pause to take a still closer look at the human misery wrought by the enslavement of women through unwilling motherhood? Would you know the appalling sum of this misery better than any author, any scientist, any physician, any social worker can tell you? Hear the story from the lips of the women themselves. Learn at first hand what it means to make a broken drudge of a woman who might have been the happy mother of a few strong children. Learn from the words of the victims of involuntary motherhood what it means to them, to their children and to society to force the physically unfit or the unwilling to bear children. When you have learned, stop to ask yourself what is the worth of the law, the moral code, the tradition, the religion, that for the sake of an outworn dogma of submission would wreck the lives of these women, condemn their progeny to pain, want, disease and helplessness. Ask yourself if these letters, these cries of despair, born of the anguish of woman's sex slavery are not in themselves enough to stop the mouths of the demagogues, the imperialists and the ecclesiastics who clamor for more and yet more children? An, d if the pain of others has no power to move your heart and stir your hands and brain to action, ask yourself the more selfish question: Can the children of these unfortunate mothers be other than a burden to society--a burden which reflects itself in innumerable phases of cost, crime and general social detriment?

"For our own sakes--for our children's sakes--" plead the mothers, "help us! Let us be women, rather than breeding machines."

The women who thus cry out are pleading not only for themselves and their children, but for society itself. Their plea is for us and ours--it is the plea for happier conditions, for higher ideals, for a stronger, more vigorous, more highly developed race.

The letters in this chapter are the voices of humble prophets crying out to us stop our national habit of human waste. They are warnings against disaster which we now share and must continue to share as it grows worse, unless we heed the warning and put our national house in order.

Each and every unwanted child is likely to be in some way a social liability. It is only the wanted child who is likely to be a social asset. If we have faith in this intuitive demand of the unfortunate mothers, if we understand both its dire and its hopeful significance, we shall dispose of those social problems which so insistently and menacingly confront us today. For the instinct of maternity to protect its own fruits, the instinct of womanhood to be free to give something besides surplus of children to the world, cannot go astray. The rising generation is always the material of progress, and motherhood is the agency for the improvement and the strengthening and guiding of that generation.

The excerpts contained in this chapter are typical of the letters which come to me by the thousands. They tell their own story, simply--sometimes ungrammatically and illiterately, but nevertheless irresistibly. It is the story of slow murder of the helpless by a society that shields itself behind ancient, inhuman moral creeds--which dares to weigh those dead creeds against the agony of the living who pray for the "mercy of death."

Can a mother who would "rather die" than bear more children serve society by bearing still others? Can children carried through nine months of dread and unspeakable mental anguish and born into an atmosphere of fear and anger, to grow up uneducated and in want, be a benefit to the world? Here is what the mother says:

"I have read in the paper about you and am very interested in Birth Control. I am a mother of four living children and one dead the oldest 10 and baby 22 months old. I am very nervous and sickly after my children. I would like you to advise me what to do to prevent from having any more as I would rather die than have another. I am keeping away from my husband as much as I can, but it causes quarrels and almost separation. All my babies have had marasmus in the first year of their lives and I almost lost my baby last summer. I always worry about my children so much. My husband works in a brass foundry it is not a very good job and living is so high that we have to live as cheap as possible. I've only got 2 rooms and kitchen and I do all my work and sewing which is very hard for me."

Shall this woman continue to be forced into a life of unnatural continence which further aggravates her ill health and produces constant discord? Shall she go on having children who come into being with a heritage of ill-health and poverty, and who are bound to become public burdens? Or would it be the better policy to let motherhood follow its instinct to save itself, its offspring and society from these ills?

Or shall women be forced into abortion, as is testified by the mother whose daughters are mothers, and who, in the hope of saving them from both slavery and the destruction of their unborn children, wrote the letter which follows:

"I have born and raised 6 children and I know all the hardships of raising a large family. I am now 53 years old and past having children but I have 3 daughters that have 2 children each and they say they will die before they will have any more and every now and again they go to a doctor and get rid of one and someday I think it will kill them but they say they don't care for they will be better dead than live in hell with a big family and nothing to raise them on. It is for there sakes I wish you to give me that information."

What could the three women mentioned in this letter contribute to the well-being of the future American race? Nothing, except by doing exactly what they wish to do--refusing to bear children that they do not want and cannot care for. Their instinct is sound--but what is to be said of the position of society at large, which forces women who are in the grip of a sound instinct to seek repeated abortions in order to follow that instinct? Are we not compelling women to choose between inflicting injury upon themselves, their children and the community, and undergoing an abhorrent operation which kills the tenderness and delicacy of womanhood, even as it may injure or kill the body?

Will the offspring of a paralytic, who must perforce neglect the physical care and training of her children, enhance the common good by their coming? Here is a letter from a paralytic mother, whose days and nights are tortured by the thought. of another child, and whose reason is tottering at the prospect of leaving her children without her care:

"I sent for a copy of your magazine and now feel I must write you to see if you can help me.

"I was a high school girl who married a day laborer seven years ago. In a few months I will again be a mother, the fourth child in less than six years. While carrying my babies am always partly paralyzed on one side. Do not know the cause but the doctor said at last birth we must be 'more careful,' as I could not stand having so many children. Am always very sick for a long time and have to have chloroform.

"We can afford help only about 3 weeks, until I am on my feet again, after confinement. I work as hard as I can but my work and my children are always neglected. I wonder if my body does survive this next birth if my reason will.

"It is terrible to think of bringing these little bodies and souls into the world without means or strength to care for them. And I can see no relief unless you give it to me or tell me where to get it. I am weaker each time and I know that this must be the last one, for it would be better for me to go, than to bring more neglected babies into the world. I can hardly sleep at night for worrying. Is there an answer for women like me?"

In another chapter, we have gotten a glimpse of the menace of the feebleminded. Here is a woman who is praying for help to avoid adding to the number of mentally helpless:

"My baby is only 10 months old and the oldest one of four is 7, and more care than a baby, has always been helpless. We do not own a roof over our heads and I am so discouraged I want to die if nothing can be done. Can't you help me just this time and then I know I can take care of myself. Ignorance on this all important subject has put me where I am. I don't know how to be sure of bringing myself around. I beg of you to help me and anything I can do to help further your wonderful work I will do. Only help me this once, no one will know only I will be blessed.

"I not only have a terrible time when I am confined but caring for the oldest child it preys so on my mind that I fear more defective children. Help me please!"

The offspring of one feebleminded man named Jukes has cost the public in one way and another $1,300,000 in seventy-five years, Do we want more such families? Is this woman standing guard for the general welfare?

Had she been permitted the use of contraceptives before she was forced to make a vain plea for abortion, would she not have rendered a service to her fellow citizens, as well as to herself?

Millions are spent in the United States every year to combat tuberculosis. The national waste involved in illness and deaths from tuberculosis runs up into the billions. Is it then good business, to say nothing of the humane aspects of the situation, to compel the writer of the following letter to go on adding to the number of the tubercular? Which is the guardian of public welfare here-- the mother instinct which wishes to avoid bearing tubercular children, or the statute which forbids her to know how to avoid adding to the census of "white plague" victims? The letter reads:

"Kindly pardon me for writing this to you, not knowing what trouble this may cause you. But I've heard of you through a friend and realize you are a friend of humanity. If people would see with your light, the world would be healthy. I married the first time when I was eighteen years old, a drinking man. I became mother to five children. In 1908 my husband died of consumption. I lost two of my oldest children from the same disease, one at 16 and the other at 23. The youngest of them all, a sweet girl of nineteen, now lies at ------ sanatorium expecting to leave us at any time. The other sister and brother look very poorly.

"I have always worked very hard, because I had to. In 1913 I married again, a good man this time, but a laboring man, and our constant fear and trouble is what may happen if we bring children into the world. I'm forty-six years old this month and not very well any more, either. So a godsend will be some one who can tell me how to care for myself, so I can be free from suffering and also not bring mortals to earth to suffer and die."

Not even the blindest of all dogmatists can ignore the danger to the community of to-day and the race of to-morrow in permitting an insane woman to go on bearing children. Here is a letter which tells a two-sided story--how mother instinct, even when clouded by periodic insanity, seeks to protect itself and society, and how society prevents her from attaining that end:

"There is a woman in this town who has six children and is expecting another. Directly after the birth of a child, she goes insane, a raving maniac, and they send her to the insane asylum. While she is gone, her home and children are cared for by neighbors. After about six months, they discharge her and she comes home and is in a family way again in a few months. Still the doctors will do nothing for her.

"She is a well-educated woman and says if she would not have any more children, she is sure she could be entirely free from these insane spells.

"If you will send me one of your pamphlets, I will give it to her and several others equally deserving.

"Hoping you will see fit to grant my request, I remain, etc.'

The very word "syphilis" brings a shudder to anyone who is familiar with the horrors of the malady. Not only in the suffering brought to the victim himself and in the danger of infecting others, but in the dire legacy of helplessness and disease which is left to the offspring of the syphilitic, is this the most destructive socially, of all "plagues." Here is a letter, which as a criticism of our present public policy in regard to national waste and to contraceptives, defies comment:

"I was left without a father when a girl of fourteen years old. I was the oldest child of five. My mother had no means of support except her two hands, so we worked at anything we could, my job being nurse girl at home while mother worked most of the time, as she could earn more money than I could, for she could do harder work.

"I wasn't very strong and finally after two years my mother got so tired and worn out trying to make a living for so many, she married again, and as she married a poor man, we children were not much better off. At the age of seventeen I married a man, a brakeman on the ------ Railroad, who was eleven years older than I. He drank some and was a very frail-looking man, but I was very ignorant of the world and did not think of anything but making a home for myself and husband. After eleven months I had a little girl born to me. I did not want more children, but my mother-in-law told me it was a terrible sin to do anything to keep from having children and that the Lord only sent just what I could take care of and if I heard of anything to do I was told it was injurious, so I did not try.

"In eleven months again, October 25, I had another little puny girl. In twenty-three months, Sept. 25th,, I had a seven-lb. boy. In ten months, July 15, I had a seven-months baby that lived five hours. In eleven months, June 20, I had another little girl. In seventeen months, Nov. 30, another boy. In nine months a four months' miscarriage. In twelve months another girl, and in three and a half years another girl.

"All of these children were born into poverty; the father's health was always poor, and when the third girl was born he was discharged from the road because of his disability, yet he was still able to put children into the world. When the oldest child was twelve years old the father died of concussion of the brain while the youngest child was born two months after his death.

"Now, Mrs. Sanger, I did not want those children, because even in my ignorance I had sense enough to know that I had no right to bring those children into such a world where they could not have decent care, for I was not able to do. it myself nor hire it done. I prayed and I prayed that they would die when they were born. Praying did no good and to-day I have read and studied enough to know that I am the another of seven living children and that I committed a crime by bringing them into the world, their father wits syphilitic (I did not know about such things when I was a girl). One son is to be sent to Mexico, while one of my girls is a victim of the white slave traffic.

"I raised my family in a little college town in ----- and am well known there, for I made my living washing and working for the college people while I raised my little brood. I often wondered why those educated well-to-do people never had so many children. I have one married daughter who is tubercular, and she also has two little girls, only a year apart. I feel so bad about it, and write to ask you to send me information for her. Don't stop your good work; don't think it's not appreciated; for there are hundreds of women like myself who are not afraid to risk their lives to help you to get this information to poor women who need it."

There is no need to go on repeating these cries. These letters have come to me by the thousands. There are enough of them to fill many volumes--each with its own individual tragedy, each with its own warning to society.

Every ill that we are trying to cure to-day is reflected in them. The wife who through an unwilling continence drives her husband to prostitution; habitual drunkenness, which prohibition may or may not have disposed of as a social problem; mothers who toil in mills and whose children must follow them to that toil, adding to the long train of evils involved in child labor; mothers who have brought eight, ten, twelve or fifteen undernourished, weakly children into the world to become public burdens of one sort or another--all these and more, with the ever-present economic problem, and women who are remaining unmarried because they fear a large family which must exist in want; men who are living abnormal lives for the same reason. All the social handicaps and evils of the day are woven into these letters--and out of each of them rises these challenging facts: First, oppressed motherhood knows that the cure for these evils lies in birth control; second, society has not yet learned to permit motherhood to stand guard for itself, its children, the common good and the coming race. And one reading such letters, and realizing their significance, is constrained to wonder how long such a situation can exist.

CHAPTER VII

WHEN SHOULD A WOMAN AVOID HAVING CHILDREN?

ARE overburdened mothers justified in their appeals for contraceptives or abortions? What shall we say to women who write such letters as those published in the preceding chapter? Will anyone, after reading those letters, dare to say to these women that they should go on bringing helpless children into the world to share their increasing misery?

The women who thus cry for aid are the victims of ignorance. Awakening from that ignorance, they are demanding relief. Had they been permitted a knowledge of their sex functions, had they had some guiding principle of motherhood, those who at this late day are asking for contraceptives would have swept aside all barriers and procured them long ago. Those who are appealing for abortions would never have been in such a situation.

To say to these women that they should continue their helpless breeding of the helpless is stupid brutality. The facts set forth earlier in this book, and the cries of tortured motherhood which echo through the letters just referred to, are more than ample evidence that there are times when it is woman's highest duty to refuse to bear children.

There has seemed to be a great deal of disagreement among the medical authorities who have attempted to say when a woman should not have children. This disagreement has been rendered even more confusing by a babel of voices from the ranks of sociologists. Within the past few years, however, so much light has been shed upon the subject that it is now comparatively easy for the student to separate the well-founded conclusions from those which are of doubtful value, or plainly worthless. The opinions which I summarize here are not so much my own, originally, as those of medical authorities who have made deep and careful investigations. There is, however, nothing set forth here which I have not in my own studies tested and proved correct. In addition to carrying the weight of the best medical authority, a fact easily confirmed by the first specialist you meet, they are further reinforced by the findings of the federal Children's Bureau, and other, organizations which have examined infant mortality and compiled rates.

To the woman who wishes to have children, we must give these answers to the question when not to have them.

Childbearing should be avoided within two or three years after the birth of the last child. Common sense and science unite in pointing out that the mother requires at least this much time to regain her strength and replenish her system in order to give another baby proper nourishment after its birth, Authorities are insistent upon their warnings that too frequent childbearing wrecks the woman's health. Weakness of the reproductive organs and pelvic ailments almost certainly result if a woman bears children too frequently.

By all means there should be no children when either mother or father suffers from such diseases as tuberculosis, gonorrhea, syphilis, cancer, epilepsy, insanity, drunkenness and mental disorders. In the case of the mother, heart disease, kidney trouble and pelvic deformities are also a serious bar to childbearing.

Thousands of volumes have been written by physicians upon the danger to mothers and offspring of having children when one or both parents are suffering from the diseases mentioned above. As authorities have pointed out in all these books, the jails, hospitals for the insane, poorhouses and houses of prostitution are filled with the children born of such parents, while an astounding number of their children are either stillborn or die in infancy.

These facts are now so well known that they would, need little discussion here, even if space permitted. Miscarriages, which are particularly frequent in cases of syphilis and pelvic deformities, are a great source of danger to the health and even to the life of the mother. Where either parent suffers from gonorrhea, the child is in danger of being born blind. Tuberculosis in the parent leaves the child's system in such condition that it is likely to suffer from the disease. Childbearing is also a grave danger to the tubercular mother. A tendency to insanity, if not insanity itself, may be transmitted to the child, or it may be feebleminded if one of the parents is insane or suffers from any mental disorder. Drunkenness in the parent or parents has been found to be the cause of feeblemindedness in the offspring and to leave the child with a constitution too weak to resist disease as it should.

No more children should be born when the parents, though healthy themselves, find that their children are physically or mentally defective. No matter how much they desire children, no man and woman have a right to bring into the world those who are to suffer from mental or physical affliction. It condemns the child to a life of misery and places upon the community the burden of caring for it, probably for its defective descendants for many generations.

Generally speaking, no woman should bear a child before she is twenty-two years old. It is better still that she wait until she is twenty-five. High infant mortality rates for mothers under twenty-two attest this fact. It is highly desirable from the mother's standpoint to postpone childbearing until she has attained a ripe physical and mental development, as the bearing and nursing of infants interferes with such development. It is also all important to the child; the offspring of a woman who is twenty-five or somewhat older has the best chance of good physical and mental equipment.

In brief, a woman should avoid having children unless both she and the father are in such physical and mental condition as to assure the child a healthy physical and mental being. This is the answer that must he made to women whose children are fairly sure of good care, sufficient food, adequate clothing, a fit place to live and at least a fair education.

A distinctly different and exceedingly important side of the problem must be considered when the women workers, the wives and the mothers of workers, wish to know when to avoid having children. Such a woman must answer her own question. What anyone else may tell her is far less important than what she herself shall reply to a society that demands more and more children and which gives them less and less when they arrive.

What shall this woman say to a society that would make of her body a reproductive machine only to waste prodigally the fruit of her being? Does society value her offspring? Does it not let them die by the hundreds of thousands of want, hunger and preventable disease? Does it not drive them to the factories, the mills, the mines and the stores to be stunted physically and mentally? Does it not throw them into the labor market to be competitors with her and their father? Do we not find the children of the South filling the mills, working side by side with their mothers, while the fathers remain at home? Do we not find the father, mother and child competing with one another for their daily bread? Does society not herd them in slums? Does it not drive the girls to prostitution and the boys to crime? Does it educate them for free-spirited manhood and womanhood? Does it even give them during their babyhood fit places to live in, fit clothes to wear, fit food to eat, or a clean place to play? Does it even permit the mother to give them a mother's care?

The woman of the workers knows what society does with her offspring. Knowing the bitter truth, learned in unspeakable anguish, what shall this woman say to society? The power is in her hands. She can bring forth more children to perpetuate these conditions, or she can withhold the human grist from these cruel mills which grind only disaster.

Shall she say to society that she will go on multiplying the misery that she herself has endured? Shall she go on breeding children who can only suffer and die? Rather, shall she not say that until society puts a higher value upon motherhood she will not be a mother? Shall she not sacrifice her mother instincts for the common good and say that until children are held as something better than commodities upon the labor market, she will bear no more? Shall she not give up her desire for even a small family, and say to society that until the world is made fit for children to live in, she will have no children at all?

CHAPTER VIII

BIRTH CONTROL--A PARENTS' PROBLEM OR WOMAN'S?

THE problem of birth control has arisen directly from the effort of the feminine spirit to free itself from bondage. Woman herself has wrought that bondage through her reproductive powers and while enslaving herself has enslaved the world. The physical suffering to be relieved is chiefly woman's. Hers, too, is the love life that dies first under the blight of too prolific breeding. Within her is wrapped up the future of the race--it is hers to make or mar. All of these considerations point unmistakably to one fact--it is woman's duty as well as her privilege to lay hold of the means of freedom. Whatever men may do, she cannot escape the responsibility. For ages she has been deprived of the opportunity to meet this obligation. She is now emerging from her helplessness. Even as no one can share the suffering of the overburdened mother, so no one can do this work for her. Others may help, but she and she alone can free herself.

The basic freedom of the world is woman's freedom. A free race cannot be born of slave mothers. A woman enchained cannot choose but give a measure of that bondage to her sons and daughters. No woman can call herself free who does not own and control her body. No woman can call herself free until she can choose consciously whether she will or will not be a mother.

It does not greatly alter the case that some women call themselves free because they earn their own livings, while others profess freedom because they defy the conventions of sex relationship. She who earns her own living gains a sort of freedom that is not to be undervalued, but in quality and in quantity it is of little account beside the untrammeled choice of mating or not mating, of being a mother or not being a mother. She gains food and clothing and shelter, at least, without submitting to the charity of her companion, but the earning of her own living does not give her the development of her inner sex urge, far deeper and more powerful in its outworkings than any of these externals. In order to have that development, she must still meet and solve the problem of motherhood.

With the so-called "free" woman, who chooses a mate in defiance of convention, freedom is largely a question of character and audacity. If she does attain to an unrestricted choice of a mate, she is still in a position to be enslaved through her reproductive powers. Indeed, the pressure of law and custom upon the woman not legally married is likely to make her more of a slave than the woman fortunate enough to marry the man of her choice.

Look at it from any standpoint you will, suggest any solution you will, conventional or unconventional, sanctioned by law or in defiance of law, woman is in the same position, fundamentally, until she is able to determine for herself whether she will be a mother and to fix the number of her offspring. This unavoidable situation is alone enough to make birth control, first of all, a woman's problem. On the very face of the matter, voluntary motherhood is chiefly the concern of the woman.

It is persistently urged, however, that since sex expression is the act of two, the responsibility of controlling the results should not be placed upon woman alone. Is it fair, it is asked, to give her, instead of the man, the task of protecting herself when she is, perhaps, less rugged in physique than her mate, and has, at all events, the normal, periodic inconveniences of her sex?

We must examine this phase of her problem in two lights--that of the ideal, and of the conditions working toward the ideal. In an ideal society, no doubt, birth control would become the concern of the man as well as the woman. The hard, inescapable fact which we encounter to-day is that man has not only refused any such responsibility, but has individually and collectively sought to prevent woman from obtaining knowledge by which she could assume this responsibility for herself. She is still in the position of a dependent to-day because her mate has refused to consider her as an individual apart from his needs. She is still bound because she has in the past left the solution of the problem to him. Having left it to him, she finds that instead of rights, she has only such privileges as she has gained by petitioning, coaxing and cozening. Having left it to him, she is exploited, driven and enslaved to his desires.

While it is true that he suffers many evils as the consequence of this situation, she suffers vastly more. While it is true that he should be awakened to the cause of these evils, we know that they come home to her with crushing force every day. It is she who bas the long burden of carrying, bearing and rearing the unwanted children. It is she who must watch beside the beds of pain where lie the babies who suffer because they have come into overcrowded homes. It is her heart that the sight of the deformed, the subnormal, the undernourished, the overworked child smites first and oftenest and hardest. It is *her* love life that dies first in the fear of undesired pregnancy. It is her opportunity for self expression that perishes first and most hopelessly because of it.

Conditions, rather than theories, facts, rather than dreams, govern the problem. They place it squarely upon the shoulders of woman. She has learned that whatever the moral responsibility of the man in this direction may be, he does not discharge it. She has learned that, lovable and considerate as the individual husband may be, she has nothing to expect from men in the mass, when they make laws and decree customs. She knows that regardless of what ought to be, the brutal, unavoidable fact is that she will never receive her freedom until she takes it for herself.

Having learned this much, she has yet something more to learn. Women are too much inclined to follow in the footsteps of men, to try to think as men think, to try to solve the general problems of life as men solve them. If after attaining their freedom, women accept conditions in the spheres of government, industry, art, morals and religion as they find them, they will be but taking a leaf out of man's book. The woman is not needed to do man's work. She is not needed to think man's thoughts. She need not fear that the masculine mind, almost universally dominant, will fail to take care of its own. Her mission is not to enhance the masculine spirit, but to express the feminine; hers is not to preserve a man-made world, but to create a human world by the infusion of the feminine element into all of its activities.

Woman must not accept; she must challenge. She must not be awed by that which has been built up around her; she must reverence that within her which struggles for expression. Her eyes must be less upon what is and more clearly upon what should be. She must listen only with a frankly questioning attitude to the dogmatized opinions of manmade society. When she chooses her new, free course of action, it must be in the light of her own opinion--of her own intuition. Only so can she give play to the feminine spirit. Only thus can she free her mate from the bondage which he wrought for himself when he wrought hers. Only thus can she restore to him that of which he robbed himself in restricting her. Only thus can she remake the world.

The world is, indeed, hers to remake, it is hers to build and to recreate. Even as she has permitted the suppression of her own feminine element and the consequent impoverishment of industry, art, letters, science, morals, religions and social intercourse, so it is hers to enrich all these.

Woman must have her freedom--the fundamental freedom of choosing whether or not she shall be a mother and how many children she will have. Regardless of what man's attitude may be, that problem is hers--and before it can be his, it is hers alone.

She goes through the vale of death alone, each time a babe is born. As it is the right neither of man nor the state to coerce her into this ordeal, so it is her right to decide whether she will endure it. That right to decide imposes upon her the duty of clearing the way to knowledge by which she may make and carry out the decision.

Birth control is woman's problem. The quicker she accepts it as hers and hers alone, the quicker will society respect motherhood. The quicker, too, will the world be made a fit place for her children to live.

CHAPTER IX

CONTINENCE--IS IT PRACTICABLE OR DESIRABLE?

THOUSANDS of well-intentioned people who agree that there are times and conditions under which it is woman's highest duty to avoid having children advocate continence as the one permissible means of birth control. Few of these people agree with one another, however, as to what continence is. Some have in mind absolute continence. Others urge continence for periods varying from a few weeks to many years. Still others are thinking of Karezza, or male continence, as it is sometimes called.

The majority of physicians and sex psychologists hold that the practice of absolute continence is, for the greater part of the human race, an absurdity. Were such continence to be practiced, there is no doubt that it would be a most effective check upon the birth rate. It is seldom practiced, however, and when adhered to under compulsion the usual result is injury to the nervous system and to the general health. Among healthy persons, this method is practicable only with those who have a degree of mentally controlled development as yet neither often experienced nor even imagined by the mass of humanity.

Absolute continence was the ideal of the early Christian church for all of its communicants, as shall be seen in another chapter. We shall also see how the church abandoned this standard and now confines the doctrine of celibacy to the unmarried, to the priesthood and the nuns.

Celibacy has been practiced in all ages by a few artists, propagandists and revolutionists in order that their minds may be single to the work which has claimed their lives and all the forces of their beings may be bent in one direction. Sometimes, too, such persons have remained celibate to avoid the burden of caring for a family.

The Rev. Dr. Thomas Robert Malthus, who in 1798 issued the first of those works which exemplified what is called the Malthusian doctrine, also advocated celibacy or absolute continence until middle age. Malthus propounded the now widely recognized principle that population tends to increase faster than the food supply and that unlimited reproduction brings poverty and many other evils upon a nation. His theological training naturally inclined him to favor continence--not so much from its practicability, perhaps, as because he believed that it was the only possible method.

We would be ignoring a vital truth if we failed to recognize the fact that there are individuals who through absorption in religious zeal, consecration to a cause, or devotion to creative work are able to live for years or for a lifetime a celibate existence. It is doubtless true that the number of those who are thus able to transmute their sex forces into other creative forms is increasing. It is not with these, however, that we are concerned. Rather it is with the mass of humanity, who practice continence under some sort of compulsion.

What is the result of forcing continence upon those who are not fitted or do not desire to practice it? The majority opinion of medical science and the evidence of statistics are united on this point. Enforced continence is injurious--often highly so.

"Physiology," writes Dr. J. Rutgers in *Rassenverbesserung*, "teaches that every function gains in power and efficiency through a certain degree of control, but that the too extended suppression of a desire gives rise to pathological disturbances and in time cripples the function. Especially in the case of women may the damage entailed by too long continued sexual abstinence bring about deep disturbances."

All this, be it understood, refers to persons of mature age. For young men and women under certain ages, statistics and the preponderance of medical opinion agree that continence is highly advisable, in many cases seemingly altogether necessary to future happiness. The famous Dr. Bertillon, of France, inventor of the Bertillon system of measurements for the human body, has made, perhaps, the most exhaustive of all studies in this direction. He demonstrates a large mortality for the boy who marries before his twentieth year. When single, the mortality of French youths averages only 14 per thousand; among married youths it rises to 100 per thousand. Which shows that it is six or eight times more perilous for a youth to be incontinent than continent up to that age. Dr. Bertillon's conclusions are that men should marry between their twenty-fifth and thirtieth years, and that women should marry when they have passed twenty. With the single exception of young men and women below the ages noted, Dr. Bertillon's statistics tell a very different story. And where it relates to celibates, it is a shocking one.

"Dr. Bertillon shows that in France, Belgium and Holland married men live considerably longer than single ones," writes Dr. Charles R. Drysdale, in summing up the matter in "*The Population Question*," "and are much less subject to becoming insane, criminal or vicious." From the same studies we learn that the conjugal state is also more favorable to the health of the woman over twenty years of age, in the three countries covered.

An analysis of criminal records showed that more than twice as many unmarried men and women had been held for crimes of all kinds than married persons. Rates based upon 10,000 cases of insanity among men and women in the same countries showed 3.95 per thousand for male celibates against 2.17 for married men. For single women the rate was 3.4 against but 1.9 for married women. Insanity was reduced one-half among women by marriage.

More startling still is the evidence of the mortality statistics. Bertillon found that the death rates of bachelors and widowers averaged from nearly two to nearly three times as high as those of married men of the same ages. Dr. Mayer, in his *Rapports Conjugaux*, showed that the death rates among the celibate religious orders studied were nearly twice as high as those of the laity.

Can anyone knowing the facts ask that we recommend continence as a birth-control measure?

Virtually all of the dangers to health involved in absolute continence are involved also in the practice of continence broken only when it is desired to bring a child into the world. In the opinion of some medical authorities, it is even worse, because of the almost constant excitation of unsatisfied sex desire by the presence of the mate.

People who think that they believe in this sort of family limitation have much to say about "self-control." Usually they will admit that to abstain from all but a single act of sexual intercourse each year is an indication of high powers of self-restraint. Yet that one act, performed only once a year, might be sufficient to "keep a woman with one child in her womb and another at her breast" during her entire childbearing period. That would mean from eighteen to twenty-four children for each mother, provided she survived so many births and lactations. Contraceptives are quite as necessary to these "self-controlled" ones who do not desire children every year as to those who lead normal, happy love lives.

From the necessity of contraceptives and from the dangers of this limited continence certain persons are, of course, relieved. They are the ones whose mental and spiritual development is so high as to make this practice natural to them. These individuals are so exceedingly rare, however, that they need not be discussed here. Moreover, they are capable of solving their own problems.

Few who advocate the doctrine of absolute continence live up to it strictly. I met one woman who assured me that she had observed it faithfully in the thirteen years since her youngest child was born. She had such a loathing for sexual union, however, that it was doubtless the easiest and best thing for her to do.

Loathing, disgust or indifference to the sex relationship nearly always lies behind the advocacy to continence except for the conscious purpose of creating children. In other words, while one in ten thousand persons may find full play for a diverted and transmuted sex force in other creative functions, the rest avoid the sex union from repression. These are two widely different situations--one may make for racial progress and the happiness of the few individuals capable of it; the other poisons the race at its fountain and brings nothing but the discontent, unhappiness and misery which follow enforced continence. For all that, an increasing number of persons, mostly women, are advocating continence within marriage.

Sexual union is nearly always spoken of by such persons as something in itself repugnant, disgusting, low and lustful. Consciously or unconsciously, they look upon it as a hardship, to be endured only, to bring "God's image and, likeness" into the world. Their very attitude precludes any great probability that their progeny will possess an abundance of such qualities.

Much of the responsibility for this feeling upon the part of many thousands of women must be laid to two thousand years of Christian teaching that all sex expression is unclean. Part of it, too, must be laid to the dominant male's habit of violating the love rights of his mate.

The habit referred to grows out of the assumed and legalized right of the husband to have sexual satisfaction at any time he desires, regardless of the woman's repugnance for it. The law of the state upholds him in this regard. A husband need not support his wife if she refuses to comply with his sexual demands.

Of the two groups of women who regard physical union either with disgust and loathing, or with indifference, the former are the less numerous.

Nevertheless, there are many thousands of them. I have listened to their stories often, both as a nurse in obstetrical cases and as a propagandist for birth control An almost universal cause of their attitude is a sad lack of understanding of the great beauties of the normal, idealistic love act. Neither do they understand the uplifting power of such unions for both men and women. Ignorance of life, ignorance of all but the sheer reproductive function of mating, and especially a wrong training, are most largely responsible for this tragic state of affairs. When this ignorance extends to the man in such a degree as to permit him to have the all too frequent coarse and brutal attitude toward sex matters, the tragedy is only deepened.

Truly the church and those "moralists" who have been insisting upon keeping sex matters in the dark have a huge list of concealed crimes to answer for. The right kind of a book, a series of clear, scientific lectures, or a common-sense talk with either the man or woman will often do away with most of the repugnance to physical union. When the repugnance is gone, the way is open to that upliftment through sex idealism which is the birthright of all women and men.

When I have had the confidence of women indifferent to physical union, I have found the fault usually lay with the husband. His idea of marriage is too often that of providing a home for a female who would in turn provide for his physical needs, including sexual satisfaction. Such a husband usually excludes such satisfaction from the category of the wife's needs, physical or spiritual.

This man is not concerned with his wife's sex urge, save as it responds to his own at times of his choosing. Man's code has taught woman to be quite ashamed of such desires. Usually she speaks of indifference without regret; often proudly. She seems to regard herself as more chaste and highly endowed in purity than other women who confess to feeling physical attraction toward their husbands. She also secretly considers herself far superior to the husband who makes no concealment of his desire toward her. Nevertheless, because of this desire upon the husband's part, she goes on "pretending" to mutual interest in the relationship.

Only the truth, plainly spoken, can help these people. The woman is condemned to physical, mental and spiritual misery by the ignorance which society has fixed upon her. She has her choice between an enforced continence, with its health-wrecking consequences and its constant aggravation of domestic discord, and the sort of prostitution legalized by the marriage ceremony. The man may choose between enforced continence and its effects, or he may resort to an unmarried relationship or to prostitution. Neither of these people--the one schooled directly or indirectly by the church and the other trained in the sex ethics of the gutter--can hope to lift the other to the regenerating influences of a pure, clean, happy love life. As long as we leave sex education to the gutter and houses of prostitution, we shall have millions of just such miserable marriage failures.

Such continence as is involved in dependence upon the so-called "safe period" for family limitation will harm no one. The difficulty here is that the method is not practical. It simply does not work. The woman who employs this method finds herself in the same predicament as the one who believes that she is not in danger of pregnancy when she does not respond passionately to her husband. That this woman is more likely to conceive than the emotional one, is a well-known fact. The woman who refuses to use contraceptives, but who rejects sex expression except for a few days in the month, is likely to learn too soon the fallacy of her theory as a birth-control method.

For a long time the "safe period" was suggested by physicians. It was also the one method of birth control countenanced by the ecclesiastics. Women are learning from experience and specialists are discovering by investigation that the "safe period" is anything but safe for all women. Some women are never free from the possibility of conception from puberty to the menopause. Others seemingly have "safe periods" for a time, only to become pregnant when they have begun to feel secure in their theory. Here again, continence must give way, as a method of birth control, to contraceptives.

In the same category as the "safe period," as a method of birth control, must be placed so-called "male continence." The same practice is also variously known as "Karezza," "Sedular Absorption" and "Zugassent's Discovery." Those who regard it as a method of family limitation are likely to find themselves disappointed.

As a form of continence, however, if it can be called continence, it is asserted to bring none of the long course of evils which too often follow the practice of lifelong abstinence, or abstinence broken only when a child is desired Its devotees testify that they avoid ill effects and achieve the highest possible results. These results are due, probably, to two factors.

First, those who practice Karezza are usually of a high mental and spiritual development and are, therefore, capable of an exalted degree of self-control without actual repression. Second, they have the benefit of that magnetic interchange between man and woman which makes for physical, mental and spiritual wellbeing. This stimulation becomes destructive irritation in ordinary forms of continence.

The Oneida Community, {sic} a religious group comprising about 130 men and 150 women, which occupied a part of an old Indian reservation in the state of New York, were the chief exponents of "male continence." The practice was a religious requirement with them and they laid great stress upon three different functions which they attributed to the sexual organs. They held that these functions were urinary, reproductive and amative, each separate {sic} and distinct in its use from the others. Cases are cited in which both men and women are said to have preserved their youth and their sexual powers to a ripe old age, and to have prolonged their honeymoons throughout married life. The theory, however, interesting as it may be when considered as "continence," is not to be relied upon as a method of birth control.

Summing it all up, then, continence may meet the needs of a few natures., but it does not meet the needs of the masses. To enforce continence upon those whose natures do not demand it, is an injustice, the cruelty and the danger of which has been underestimated rather than exaggerated. It matters not whether this wrong is committed by the church, through some outworn dogma; by the state through the laws prohibiting contraceptives, or by society, through the conditions which prevent marriage when young men and women reach the age at which they have need of marriage.

The world has been governed too long by repression. The more fundamental the force that is repressed the more destructive its action. The disastrous effects of repressing the sex force are written plainly in the health rates, the mortality statistics, the records of crime and the entry books of the hospitals for the insane. Yet this is not all the tale, for there are still the little understood hosts of sexually abnormal people and the monotonous misery of millions who do not die early nor end violently, but who are, nevertheless, devoid of the joys of a natural love life.

As a means of birth control, continence is as impracticable for most people as it is undesirable. Celibate women doubtless have their place in the regeneration of the world, but it is not they, after all, who will, through experience and understanding recreate it. It is mainly through fullness of expression and experience in life that the mass of women, having attained freedom, will accomplish this unparalleled task.

The need of women's lives is not repression, but the greatest possible expression and fulfillment of their desires upon the highest possible plane. They cannot reach higher planes through ignorance and compulsion. They can attain them only through knowledge and the cultivation of a higher, happier attitude toward sex. Sex life must be stripped of its fear. This is one of the great functions of contraceptives. That which is enshrouded in fear becomes morbid. That which is morbid cannot be really beautiful.

A true understanding of every phase of the love life, and such an understanding alone, can reveal it in its purity--in its power of up liftment. Force and fear have failed from the beginning of time. Their fruits are wrecks and wretchedness. Knowledge and freedom to choose or reject the sexual embrace, according as it is lovely or unlovely, and these alone, can solve the problem. These alone make possible between man and woman that indissoluble tie and mutual passion, and common understanding, in which lies the hope of a higher race.

CHAPTER X

CONTRACEPTIVES OR ABORTION?

SOCIETY has not yet learned the significance of the age-long effort of the feminine spirit to free itself of the burden of excessive childbearing. It has been singularly blind to the real forces underlying the cause of infanticide, child abandonment and abortion. It has permitted the highest and most powerful thing in woman's nature to be hindered, diverted, repressed and confused. Society has permitted this inner urge of woman to be rendered violent by repression until it has expressed itself in cruel forms of family limitation, which this same society has promptly labeled "crimes" and sought to punish. It has gone on blindly forcing women into these "crimes," deaf alike to their entreaties and to the lessons of history.

As we have seen in the second chapter of this book, child abandonment and infanticide are by no means obsolete practices.

As for abortion, it has not decreased but increased with the advance of civilization. The reader will recall that one authority says that there are 1,000,000 abortions in the United States every year, while another estimates double that number.

Most of the women of the middle and upper classes in America seem secure in their knowledge of contraceptives as a means of birth control. Under present conditions, when the laws in most states regard this knowledge, howsoever it be imparted, as illicit, and the federal statutes prohibit the sending of it through the mails, even the women in more fortunate circumstances sometimes have difficulty in getting scientific information. Nevertheless, so strong is their purpose that they do obtain it and use it, correctly or incorrectly.

The great majority of women, however, belong to the working class. Nearly all of these women will fall into one of two general groups--the ones who are having children against their wills, and those who, to escape this evil, find refuge in abortion. Being given their choice by society--to continue to be overburdened mothers or to submit to a humiliating, repulsive, painful and too often gravely dangerous operation, those women in whom the feminine urge to freedom is strongest choose the abortionist. One group goes on bringing children to birth, hoping that they will be born dead or die. The women of the other group strive consciously by drastic means to protect themselves and the children already born.

"Our examinations," says Dr. Max Hirsch, an authority on the subject, "have informed us that the largest number of abortions (in the United States) are performed on married women. This fact brings us to the conclusion that contraceptive measures among the upper classes and the practice of abortion among the lower class, are the real means employed to regulate the number of offspring."

Thus a high percentage of women in comfortable circumstances escape overbreeding by the use of contraceptives. A similarly high percentage of women not in comfortable circumstances are forced to submit to forced maternity, because their only alternative at present is abortion. When accidental conception takes place, some women of both classes resort to abortion if they can obtain the services of an abortionist.

When society holds up its hands in horror at the "crime" of abortion, it forgets at whose door the first and principal responsibility for this practice rests. Does anyone imagine that a woman would submit to abortion if not denied the knowledge of scientific, effective contraceptives? Does anyone believe that physicians and midwives who perform abortions go from door to door soliciting patronage? The abortionist could not continue his practice for twenty-four hours if it were not for the fact that women come desperately begging for such operations. He could not stay out of jail a day if women did not so generally approve of his services as to hold his identity an open but seldom-betrayed secret.

The question, then, is not whether family limitation should be practiced. It *is* being practiced; it has been practiced for ages and it will always be practiced. The question that society must answer is this: Shall family limitation be achieved through birth control or abortion?

Shall normal, safe, effective contraceptives be employed, or shall we continue to force women to the abnormal, often dangerous surgical operation?

This question, too, the church, the state and the moralist must answer. The knowledge of contraceptive methods may yet for a time be denied to the woman of the working class, but those who are responsible for denying it to her, and she herself, should understand clearly the dangers to which she is exposed because of the laws which force her into the hands of the abortionist.

To understand the more clearly the difference between birth control by contraceptives and family limitation through abortion it is necessary to know something of the processes of conception. Knowledge of these processes will also enable us to comprehend more thoroughly the dangers to which woman is exposed by our antiquated laws, and how much better it would be for her to employ such preventive measures as would keep her out of the hands of the abortionist, into which the laws now drive her.

In every woman's ovaries are imbedded millions of ovules or eggs. They are in every female at birth, and as the girl develops into At a womanhood, these ovules develop also. At a certain age, varying slightly with the individual, the ripest ovule leaves the nest or ovary and comes down one of the tubes connecting with the womb and passes out of the body. When this takes place, it is said that the girl is at the age of puberty. When it reaches the womb the ovule is ready for the process of conception--that is, fertilization by the male sperm.

At the time the ovule is ripening, the womb is preparing to receive it. This preparation consists of a reinforced blood supply brought to its lining. If fertilization takes place, the fertilized ovule or ovum will cling to the lining of the womb and there gather its nourishment. If fertilization does not take place, the ovum passes out of the body and the uterus throws off its surplus blood supply. This is called the menstrual period. It occurs about once a month or every twenty-eight days.

In the male organs there are glands called testes. They secrete a fluid called the semen. In the semen is the life-giving principle called the sperm.

When intercourse takes place, if no preventive is employed, the semen is deposited in the woman's vagina. The ovule is not in the vagina, but is in the womb, farther up, or perhaps in the tube on its way to the womb. As steel is attracted to the magnet, the sperm of the male starts on its way to seek the ovum. Several of these sperm cells start, but only one enters the ovum and is absorbed into it. This process is called fertilization, conception or impregnation.

If no children are desired, the meeting of the male sperm and the ovum must be prevented. When scientific means are employed to prevent this meeting, one is said to practice birth control. The means used is known as a contraceptive.

If, however, a contraceptive is not used and the sperm meets the ovule and development begins, any attempt at removing it or stopping its further growth is called abortion.

There is no doubt that women are apt to look upon abortion as of little consequence and to treat it accordingly. An abortion is as important a matter as a confinement and requires as much attention as the birth of a child at its full term,

"The immediate dangers of abortion," says Dr. J. Clifton Edgar, in his book, "*The Practice of Obstetrics*," "are hemorrhage, retention of an adherent placenta, sepsis, tetanus, perforation of the uterus. They also cause sterility, anemia, malignant diseases, displacements, neurosis, and endometritis."

In plain, everyday language, in an abortion there is always a very serious risk to the health and often to the life of the patient.

It is only the women of wealth who can afford the best medical skill, care and treatment both at the time of the operation and afterwards. In this way they escape the usual serious consequences.

The women whose incomes are limited and who must continue at work before they have recovered from the effects of an abortion are the great army of sufferers. It is among such that the deaths due to abortion usually ensue. It is these, too, who are most often forced to resort to such operations.

If death does not result, the woman who has undergone an abortion is not altogether safe from harm. The womb may not return to its natural size, but remain large and heavy, tending to fall away from its natural position. Abortion often leaves the uterus in a condition to conceive easily again and unless prevention is strictly followed another pregnancy will surely occur. Frequent abortions tend to cause barrenness and serious, painful pelvic ailments. These and other conditions arising from such operations are very likely to ruin a woman's general health.

While there are cases where even the law recognizes an abortion as justifiable if recommended by a physician, I assert that the hundreds of thousands of abortions performed in America each year are a disgrace to civilization.

The effects of such operations upon a woman, serious as they may be, are nothing as compared to the injury done her general health by drugs taken to produce the same result. Even such drugs as are prescribed by physicians have harmful effects, and nostrums recommended by druggists are often worse still.

Even more drastic may be the effect upon the unborn child, for many women fill their systems with poisonous drugs during the first weeks of their pregnancy, only to decide at last, when drugs have failed, as they usually do, to bring the child to birth.

There are no statistics, of course, by which we may compute the amount of suffering to mother and child from the use of such drugs, but we know that the total of physical weakness and disease must be astounding. We know that the woman's own system feels the strain of these drugs and that the embryo is usually poisoned by them. The child is likely to be rickety, have heart trouble, kidney disorder, or to be generally weak in its powers of resistance.

If it does not die before it reaches its first year, it is probable that it will have to struggle against some of these weaknesses until its adolescent period.

It needs no assertion of mine to call attention to the grim fact that the laws prohibiting the imparting of information concerning the preventing of conception are responsible for tens of thousands of deaths each year in this country and an untold amount of sickness and sorrow. The suffering and the death of these women is squarely upon the heads of the lawmakers and the puritanical, masculine-minded person who insist upon retaining the abominable legal restrictions.

Try as they will they cannot escape the truth, nor hide it under the cloak of stupid hypocrisy. If the laws against imparting knowledge of scientific birth control were repealed, nearly all of the 1,000,000 or 2,000,000 women who undergo abortions in the United States each year would escape the agony of the surgeon's instruments and the long trail of disease, suffering and death which so often follows.

"He who would combat abortion," says Dr. Hirsch, "and at the same time combat contraceptive measures may be likened to the person who would fight contagious diseases and forbid disinfection. For contraceptive measures are important weapons in the fight against abortion.

"America has a law since 1873 which prohibits by criminal statute the distribution and regulation of contraceptive measures. It follows, therefore, that America stands at the head of all nations in the huge number of abortions."

There is the case in a nutshell. Family limitation will always be practiced as it is now being practiced--either by birth control or by abortion. We know that. The one means health and happiness--a stronger, better race. The other means disease, suffering, death.

The woman who goes to the abortionist's table is not a criminal but a martyr--a martyr to the bitter, unthinkable conditions brought about by the blindness of society at large. These conditions give her the choice between the surgeon's instruments and the sacrificing of what is highest and holiest in her--her aspiration to freedom, her desire to protect the children already hers. These conditions--not the woman--outface society with this question:

"Contraceptives or Abortion--which shall it be?"

CHAPTER XI

ARE PREVENTIVE MEANS CERTAIN?

THERE are several means of preventing conception which are both certain and harmless. What those means are the state laws forbid me to say. If I should defy the state laws and name those contraceptives, the federal laws would forbid this book's going through the mails. Nor can I, without coming into conflict with the laws, tell why these means are reliable. It is difficult to discuss the subject without using franker language than the statutes permit, and I do not wish to violate the law in this particular book.

"Can I rely upon this? Is it certain? Will it prevent absolutely?" Such questions, always asked by women who seek advice concerning contraceptives, testify both to their fear of involuntary motherhood and their doubt as to any and all means offered for their deliverance.

Doubt as to the certainty of contraceptives arises from two sources. One is the uninformed element in the medical profession. A physician who belongs to this element may object to birth control upon general grounds, or he may repeat old-fashioned objections to cover his ignorance of contraceptives. For, strange as it may seem, there is an amazing ignorance among physicians of this supremely important subject. The uninformed objector often assumes to speak with the voice of authority, asserting that there are no thoroughly dependable contraceptives that are not injurious to the user.

The other source of distrust is the experience of the woman herself. Having no place to go for scientific advice, she gathers her information from neighbors and friends. One offers this suggestion, another offers that, each urging the means that she has found successful and condemning others. All this is very confusing and extremely disturbing to the woman who, for one reason or another, is living in constant fear of pregancy. {sic}

It is not at all surprising that such a state of affairs exists. There has been so much secrecy about the whole subject and so much dependence upon amateurish and nonprofessional advice that it is almost impossible for anyone to procure reliable information or to recognize it when given. This is especially true in the United States where there are both federal and state laws to punish those who disseminate knowledge of birth-control methods.

Even under present conditions, however, there is a certain amount of reliable information concerning methods of birth control. We know that there are several methods of prevention which are not only dependable, but which can be used without injury either to the man or the woman. Knowledge of what these methods are and how to apply them should be available to every married man and woman. It is safe to predict that in a very few years they will be available.

Some methods are more dependable than others, just as there are some more simple of adjustment than others. Some are cheap and less durable; others are expensive and last for years. There are some which for a quarter of a century have stood the test of certainty in Holland, France, England and the United States among the wealthier classes, as the falling birth rate among these classes indicates. And just as the reliable, primitive wheelbarrow is antiquated beside the latest airplane, so, as scientific investigators turn their attention more and more to this field, will the awkward, troublesome methods of the past give way to the simpler, more convenient methods of the morrow.

Although the law forbids information concerning reliable means of contraception, it is hardly likely that it can be invoked to prevent warnings against widely practiced methods which are NOT reliable. The employment of such methods leads not only to disappointment but often to ill health.

One of the most common practices of this kind is that of nursing one baby too long in the hope of preventing the birth of the next. The "poor whites" of the South and many of the foreign-born women of the United States pin their hopes to this method. Often they persist in nursing a child until it is eighteen months old--almost always until they become pregnant again.

Prolonged nursing hurts both child and mother, it is said. In the child it causes a tendency to brain disease, probably through disordered digestion and nutrition. In the mother it causes a strong tendency to deafness and blindness. If a child is nursed after it is twelve months old, it is generally pale, flabby and unhealthy, often rickety, one authority points out, while the mother is usually nervous, emaciated and hysterical. If pregnancy occurs under these conditions, the mother not only injures her own health but that of the next child, often developing in it a weakness of constitution which it never overcomes.

Moreover, prolonged nursing has been found to be unreliable as a contraceptive. We know this upon good authority. It should not be depended upon at all.

In the same class is the so-called "safe period" referred to in another chapter. For many women there is never any "safe period." Others have "safe periods" for a number of years, only to find themselves pregnant because these periods have ceased without warning.

One of the most frequent of all the mistakes made in recommending contraceptives is the advice to use an antiseptic or cold-water douche. This error seems to be surprisingly persistent. I am particularly surprised to hear from women that such douches have been prescribed by physicians. Any physician who knows the first rudiments of physiology and anatomy must also know that necessary and important as an antiseptic douche is as a cleanser and hygienic measure, it is assuredly not to be advised as a means of preventing conception.

A woman may, and often does, become pregnant before she can make use of a douche. This is particularly likely to happen if her uterus is low. And the woman who does much walking, who stands for long hours or who uses the sewing machine a great deal is likely to have a low uterus. It is then much easier for the spermatazoa {sic} to enter almost directly into the womb than it would otherwise be, and the douche, no matter how soon it is used, is likely to be ineffective. The tendency of the uterus to drop under strain goes far to explain why some women who have depended upon the douche for years suddenly find themselves pregnant. Do not depend upon the douche. As a cleansing agent, it is a necessary part of every woman's toilet, but it is not a preventive.

Even if the douche were dependable, the absence of sanitary convenience from households in remote districts and the difficulty of using a douche in crowded tenements would prevent many women from making use of it.

Despite the unreliability of some methods and the harmfulness of some others, there are methods which are both harmless and certain. This much the woman who is seeking means of limiting her family may be told here. In using any method, whatsoever, all depends upon the care taken to use it properly.

No surgeon, no matter how perfect his instruments, would expect perfect results from the simplest operation did he not exercise the greatest possible care. Common sense, good judgment and taking pains are necessary in the use of all contraceptives.

More and more perfect means of preventing conception will be developed as women insist upon them. Every woman should make it plain to her physician that she expects him to be informed upon this subject. She should refuse to accept evasive answers. An increasing demand upon physicians will inevitably result in laboratory researches and experimentation. Such investigation is indeed already beginning and we may expect great progress in contraceptive methods in the near future. We may also expect more authoritative opinions upon preventive methods and devices. When women confidently and insistently demand them, they will have access to contraceptives which are both certain and harmless.

CHAPTER XII

WILL BIRTH CONTROL HELP THE CAUSE OF LABOR?

LABOR seems instinctively to have recognized the fact that its servitude springs from numbers. Seldom, however, has it applied its knowledge logically and thoroughly. The basic principle of craft unionism is limitation of the number of workers in a given trade. This has been labor's most frequent expedient for righting its wrongs. Every unionist knows, as a matter of course, that if that number is kept small enough, his organization can compel increases of wages, steady employment and decent working conditions. Craft unionism has succeeded in attaining these insofar as it has been able to apply this principle. It has failed insofar as it has been unable to apply it.

The weakness of craft unionism is that it does not carry its principle far enough. It applies its policy of limitation of numbers only to the trade. In his home, the worker, whether he is a unionist or non-unionist, goes on producing large numbers of children to compete with him eventually in the labor market.

"The history of labor," says Teresa Billington-Greig in the *Common Sense of The Population Question*;" is the history of an ever unsuccessful effort upon the part of man to bring his productive ability as a worker up to his reproductive ability. It has been a losing battle all the way."

The small percentage of highly skilled, organized workers lead in the struggle for better conditions. Craft unions, by limiting the number of men available for any one trade, manage to procure better pay, shorter hours and other advantages for their members.

Disaster, in the form of famine, pestilence, tidal waves, earthquakes or war, sometimes limits the number of available workers. Then those who live in parts of the world that are not affected, or who stay at home during wars, reap a temporary advantage.

These advantages, however, are quickly offset by increased prices, or by competition for jobs when soldiers return from war. This form of limitation of numbers works to the advantage of labor as long as it is available, but great disasters are not constantly in operation while the worker's reproductive ability is. So in a few years they have lost what nature's destructiveness won for them.

The great mass of the workers--including children and women--are unskilled and unorganized. Not only that, they are for some considerable part of the time seeking employment. They are, of course, poorly paid. Thus, through their low wages and their seeking of employment, they always come into direct competition with one another and with the skilled and organized workmen. As their families live in want and are often diseased, they create the chief social problems of the day. They bring children into the world as fast as women can bear them. With each child they increase their own misery and provide another worker to force down wages and prolong hours, through competition for employment.

This has been the way of labor from the beginning. It is labor's way in every country. Having discovered that there is no relief in legislation, labor organizes to limit its numbers in certain trades. Meanwhile the women of the working class go on breeding more workers to wipe out in the future the advantages gained for the present. In Paris, for instance, the proletarian quarters of the city show a birth rate more than three times as high as the birth rate in the well-to-do sections.

Dr. Jacques Bartillon furnishes us with statistics which prove that the birth rate in any quarter of Paris is in inverse ratio to its degree of affluence," says G. Hardy in *How to Prevent Pregnancy*. The rich Champs-Elysees has a birth rate a third of that Bellerville or of the Buttes-Chaumont. From 1,000 women from the age of fifteen to fifty, Menimontant gives 116 births; the Champs-Elysees thirty-four births.

"It is the same in Berlin. For 1,000 women from the age of fifteen to that of fifty, a very poor quarter gives 157 births; a rich quarter gives 47 births."

And so it is the world over. The very word proletarian," as Hardy points out, "means producer of children."

The children thus carelessly produced undermine the health of the mother, deepen the family's poverty, destroy the happiness of the home, and dishearten the father; all this in addition to being future competitors in the labor market. Too often their increasing number drives the mother herself into industry, where her beggarly wages tend to lower the level of those of her husband.

The first sickening feature of this general situation is the high infant mortality among the children of the workers. Many children come merely to sap the strength of the mother, suffer and die, leaving to show for their coming and going only an increased burden of sorrow and debt. The lower the family income, the more of these babies die before they are a year old.

A survey of infant mortality in Johnstown, Pa., by the federal Children's Bureau, gave these typical results for the year 1911:

Father's Earnings	Infant Mortality Rate
Under $521	197.3
$521 to $624	193.1
$625 to $779	163.1
$780 to $899	168.1
$900 to $1,199	142.3
$1,200 or over	102.
Ample	88.

These figures do not represent the total income of all families. Neither will money buy as much in 1920 as it did in 1911. Seventy per cent of the people of the United States have incomes of less than $1,000. This means that from 142 to 197 children born into such families die before they are one year old. The births and deaths of these children represent just so much useless burden of anguish and sorrow to the workers.

Despite this high infant death rate, the workers of the United States still have more children than they can care for. There are enough of them left over to provide 3,000,000 child laborers, who by working for a pittance crowd their parents out of employment and force the families deeper into poverty.

When all is said and done, the workers who produce large families have themselves to blame for the hundreds of thousands of unemployed grasping for jobs, for the strike breakers, for the policemen who beat up and arrest strikers and for the soldiers who shoot strikers down. All these come from the families of workingmen. Their fathers and mothers are workers for wages. Out of the loins of labor they come into the world and compel surplus labor to betray labor that is employed.

Nor is this all. When a workman of superior strength and skill, protected by his union, manages to maintain a large or moderate sized family in a degree of comfort, there always comes a time when he must strike to preserve what he has won. If he is not beaten by unorganized workers who seek his job, he still has to face the possibility of listening to the cries of several hungry children. If the strike is a long one, these cries often down the promptings of loyalty and class interest--often they defeat him when nothing else could.

Is it any wonder that under handicaps like these labor becomes confused and flounders? It has been offered a multitude of remedies--political reforms, wage legislation, statutory regulation of hours, and so on. It has been invited to embrace craft and industrial unionism, syndicalism, anarchism, socialism as panaceas for its liberation. Except in a few countries, it has not attained to aggressive power, but has been a tool for unscrupulous politicians.

Even with the temporary advantages gained by the wiping out of millions of workers in the Great War, labor's problem remains unsolved. It has now, as always, to contend with the crop of young laborers coming into the market, and with the ever-present "labor-saving" machine which, instead of relieving the worker's situation, makes it all the harder for him to escape. Fewer laborers are needed to-day for a given amount of production and distribution than before the invention of these machines. Yet, owing to the increase in the number of the workers, labor finds itself enslaved instead of liberated by the machine.

"Hitherto," says John Stuart Mill, "it is questionable if all the mechanical inventions yet made have lightened the day's toil of any human being. They have enabled a greater population to live the same life of drudgery and imprisonment, and an increased number of manufacturers and others to make fortunes."

That, in a few words, sums up the greater part of labor's progress. We blame capitalism and its wasteful, brutal industrial system for all our social problems, but our numbers were vast and our bondage grievous before modern industry came into existence. We may curse the trusts, but our subjection was accomplished before the trusts had emerged from the brain of evolution. We may blame public officials and individual employers, but our burdens were crushing before these were born. We look now here, now there, for the cause of our condition--everywhere but at the one to blame. We fight again and again for our rights, only to be conquered by our own kind, our own children, our brother's, our neighbor's

Let us carry to its logical conclusion the principle of limitation which has been partially applied by labor unions. The way to get rid of labor problems, unemployment, low wages, the surplus, unwanted population, is to stop breeding. They come from our own ranks--from our own families. The way to get better wages, shorter hours, a new system for the advancement of labor, is to make labor's numbers fewer. Let us not wait for war, famine and plague to do it. Let us cease bringing unwanted children into the world to suffer a while, add to our burdens and die. Let us cease bringing others into the world to compete with us for a living. Let the women workers practice birth control.

What are the concrete things which the worker can gain at once through birth control? First, a small family can live much better than a large one upon the wages now received. Workers could be better fed, clothed and educated. Again, fewer children in the families of the workers would tend to check the rise in the prices of food, which are forced up as the demand increases. Within a few years it would reduce the number of workers competing for jobs. The worker could the more easily force society to give him more of the product of his labor--or all of it. And while these things are taking place, the slums, with their disease, their moral degradation and all their sordid accompaniments, would automatically disappear. No worker would need to live in such tenements--hence they would be modernized or torn down. At the same time, the few children that were being born to the workers would be stronger, healthier, more courageous. They would be fit human beings--not miserable victims of murderous conditions.

Birth control does not propose to replace any of the idealistic movements and philosophies of the workers. It is not a substitute, it precedes. It is of itself a principle that lifts the heaviest of the burdens that afflict labor. It can and it must be the foundation upon which any permanently successful improvement in conditions is attained. It is, therefore, a necessary prelude in all effective propaganda.

A few years of systematic agitation for birth control would put labor in a position to solve all its problems. Labor, organized or unorganized, must take heed of this fact. Groups and parties working for a new social order must include it in their programmes. No social system, no workers' democracy, no Socialist republic can operate successfully and maintain its ideals unless the practice of birth control is encouraged to a marked and efficient degree.

In Spain I saw a bull fight. It was in the great arena at Barcelona. As bull after bull went down, his magnificent, defeated strength bleeding away through wounds inflicted by his weak but skillful assailant, I thought of the world of workers and their oppressors.

As each bull was sent into the arena, he was confronted by one assailant and twenty confusers. There was but one enemy for him to face, but there were twenty brilliant flags, each of a different color, to distract his attention from the man who held the weapon. No sooner was his real antagonist in danger, than one of the confusers fluttered a flag before his anger-maddened eyes. With one toss of his horns he could have ripped the life from the toreador, but his confusers were always there with the flags. One after another he charged them, only to spend the force of his lunges in the empty air. He found that as he was about to toss one of his confusers into the air, he was confronted by another flag, which he charged with equal futility.

Finally, utterly bewildered and exhausted, too spiritless to meet the attack, he falls under the sword thrust of the toreador. And the sun shines in the deep blue overhead, the band plays, the ten thousand gayly-clad spectators shout, while the victim is dragged out to make room for another.

It is the drama of labor.

It will be the drama of labor until labor finds its real enemy. That enemy is the reproductive ability of the working class which gluts the channels of progress with the helpless and weak, and stimulates the tyrants of the world in their oppression of mankind.

CHAPTER XIII

BATTALIONS OF UNWANTED BABIES THE CAUSE OF WAR

IN every nation of militaristic tendencies we find the reactionaries demanding a higher and still higher birth rate. Their plea is, first, that great armies are needed to *defend* the country from its possible enemies; second, that a huge population is required to assure the country its proper place among the powers of the world. At bottom the two pleas are the same.

As soon as the country becomes overpopulated, these reactionaries proclaim loudly its moral right to expand. They point to the huge population, which in the name of patriotism they have previously demanded should be brought into being. Again pleading patriotism, they declare that it is the moral right of the nation to take by force such room as it needs. Then comes war--usually against some nation supposed to be less well prepared than the aggressor.

Diplomats make it their business to conceal the facts, and politicians violently denounce the politicians of other countries. There is a long beating of tom-toms by the press and all other agencies for influencing public opinion. Facts are distorted and lies invented until the common people cannot get at the truth. Yet, when the war is over, if not before, we always find that "a place in the sun," "a path to the sea," "a route to India" or something of the sort is at the bottom of the trouble. These are merely other names for expansion.

The "need of expansion" is only another name for overpopulation. One supreme example is sufficient to drive home this truth. That the Great War, from the horror of which we are just beginning to emerge, had its source in overpopulation is too evident to be denied by any serious student of current history.

For the past one hundred years most of the nations of Europe have been piling up terrific debts to humanity by the encouragement of unlimited numbers. The rulers of these nations and their militarists have constantly called upon the people to breed, breed, breed! Large populations meant more people to produce wealth, more people to pay taxes, more trade for the merchants, more soldiers to protect the wealth. But more people also meant need of greater food supplies, an urgent and natural need for expansion.

As shown by C. V. Drysdale's famous "War Map of Europe," the great conflict began among the high birth rate countries--Germany, with its rate of 31.7, Austria-Hungary with 33.7 and 36.7, respectively, Russia with 45.4, Serbia with 38.6. Italy with her 38.7 came in, as the world is now well informed through the publication of secret treaties by the Soviet government of Russia, upon the promise of territory held by Austria. England, owing to her small home area, is cramped with her comparatively low birth rate of 26.3. France, among the belligerents, is conspicuous for her low birth rate of 19.9, but stood in the way of expansion of high birth rate Germany. Nearly all of the persistently neutral countries--Holland, Denmark, Norway, Sweden and Switzerland have low birth rates, the average being a little over 26.

Owing to the part Germany played in the war, a survey of her birth statistics is decidedly illuminating. The increase in the German birth rate up to 1876 was great. Though it began to decline then, the decline was not sufficient to offset the tremendous increase of the previous years. There were more millions to produce children, so while the average number of births per thousand was somewhat smaller, the net increase in population was still huge. From 41,000,000 in 1871, the year the Empire was founded, the German population grew to approximately 67,000,000 in 1918. Meanwhile her food supply increased only a very small per cent. In 1910, Russia had a birth rate even higher than Germany's had ever been--a little less than 48 per thousand. When czarist Russia wanted an outlet to the Mediterranean by way of Constantinople, she was thinking of her increasing population. Germany was thinking of her increasing population when she spoke as with one voice of a "place in the sun."

"For some decades," said the Royal Prussian Journal, in an article quoted by the Malthusian (London) of April 15, 1911, "the great growth of German population has been almost entirely forced into the towns, since of the four millions of increase in five years, only a few can find places in agriculture, as most properties are too small to permit of letting off a portion. And as regards the larger farms, the tendency of modern, cheaper machine methods is rather to produce a saving of the more costly manual labor.

"For some time past Germany has no longer been in the position of feeding her own population, and large quantities of food as raw-materials have to be imported, for which exports have to be exchanged. It is doubtful whether even this can for long keep pace with the present rate of increase of population."

There were other utterances which just as frankly acknowledged that, having produced surplus population, Germany proposed to procure by means of war the expansion necessary to care for it. Adelyne More, in "Uncontrolled Breeding," a study of the birth rate in its relation to war, quoted the Berliner Post: "Can a great and rapidly growing nation like Germany always renounce all claims to further development or to the expansion of its political power? The final settlement with France and England, the expansion of our colonial possessions, in order to create new German homes for the overflow of our population--these are problems which must be faced in the near future." This was published in 1913.

Just as frank was the recognition of the true cause of international conflicts by a number of British authorities.

In "Uncontrolled Breeding," the author quotes the British National Commission's report on The Declining Birth Rate: "The pressure of population in any country brings, as a chief historic consequence, overflows and migrations not only for peaceful settlement, but for conquest and for the subjugation and exploitation of weaker peoples. This always remains a chief cause of international disputes."

The militaristic claim for Germany's right to new territory was simply a claim to the right of life and food for the German babies--the same right that a chick claims to burst its shell. If there had not been other millions of people claiming the same right, there would have been no war. But there were other millions.

The German rulers and leaders pointed out the fact that expansion meant more business for German merchants, more work for German workmen at better wages, and more opportunities for Germans abroad. They also pointed out that lack of expansion meant crowding and crushing at home, hard times, heavy burdens, lack of opportunity for Germans, and what not. In this way, they gave the people of the Empire a startling and true picture of what would happen from over-crowding. Once they realized the facts, the majority of Germans naturally welcomed the so-called war of defense.

The argument was sound. Once the German mothers had submitted to the plea for overbreeding, it was inevitable that imperialistic Germany should make war. Once the battalions of unwanted babies came into existence--babies whom the mothers did not want but which they bore as a "patriotic duty"--it was too late to avoid international conflict. The great crime of imperialistic Germany was its high birth rate. It has always been so. Behind all war has been the pressure of population. "Historians," says Huxley, "point to the greed and ambition of rulers, the reckless turbulence of the ruled, to the debasing effects of wealth and luxury, and to the devastating wars which have formed a great part of the occupation of mankind, as the causes of the decay of states and the foundering of old civilizations, and thereby point their story with a moral. But beneath all this superficial turmoil lay the deep-seated impulse given by unlimited multiplication."

Robert Thomas Malthus, formulator of the doctrine which bears his name, pointed out, in the closing years of the eighteenth century, the relation of overpopulation to war. He showed that mankind tends to increase faster than the food supply. He demonstrated that were it not for the more common diseases, for plague, famine, floods and wars, human beings would crowd each other to such an extent that the misery would be even greater than it now is. These be described as "natural checks," pointing out that as long as no other checks are employed, such disasters are unavoidable. {p. 159} If we do not exercise sufficient judgment to regulate the birth rate, we encounter disease, starvation and war.

Both Darwin and John Stuart Mill recognized, by inference at least, the fact that so-called "natural checks"--and among them war--will operate if some sort of limitation is not employed. In his *Origin of Species*, Darwin says: "There is no exception to the rule that every organic being naturally increases at so high a rate, if not destroyed, that the earth would soon be covered by the progeny of a single pair." Elsewhere he observes that we do not permit helpless human beings to die off, but we create philanthropies and charities, build asylums and hospitals and keep the medical profession busy preserving those who could not otherwise survive. John Stuart Mill, supporting the views of Malthus, speaks to exactly the same effect in regard to the multiplying power of organic beings, among them humanity. In other words, let countries become overpopulated and war is inevitable. It follows as daylight follows the sunrise.

When Charles Bradlaugh and Mrs. Annie Besant were on trial in England in 1877 for publishing information concerning contraceptives, Mrs. Besant put the case bluntly to the court and the jury:

"I have no doubt that if natural checks were allowed to operate right through the human as they do in the animal world, a better result would follow. Among the brutes, the weaker are driven to the wall, the diseased fall out in the race of life. The old brutes, when feeble or sickly, are killed. If men insisted that those who were sickly should be allowed to die without help of medicine or science, if those who are weak were put upon one side and crushed, if those who were old and useless were killed, if those who were not capable of providing food for themselves were allowed to starve, if all this were done, the struggle for existence among men would be as real as it is among brutes and would doubtless result in the production of a higher race of men.

"But are you willing to do that or to allow it to be done?"

We are not willing to let it be done. Mother hearts cling to children, no matter how diseased, misshapen and miserable. Sons and daughters hold fast to parents, no matter how helpless. We do not allow the weak to depart; neither do we cease to bring more weak and helpless beings into the world. Among the dire results is war, which kills off, not the weak and the helpless. but the strong and the fit.

What shall be done? We have our choice of one of three policies. We may abandon our science and leave the weak and diseased to die, or kill them, as the brutes do. Or we may go on overpopulating the earth and have our famines and our wars while the earth exists. Or we can accept the third, sane, sensible, moral and practicable plan of birth control. We can refuse to bring weak, the helpless and the unwanted children into the world. We can refuse to overcrowd families, nations and the earth. There are these ways to meet the situation, and only these three ways.

The world will never abandon its preventive and curative science; it may be expected to elevate and extend it beyond our present imagination. The efforts to do away with famine and the opposition to war are growing by leaps and bounds. Upon these efforts are largely based our modern social revolutions.

There remains only the third expedient--birth control, the real cure for war. This fact was called to the attention of the Peace Conference in Paris, in 1919, by the Malthusian League, which adopted the following resolution at its annual general meeting in London in June of that year:

"The Malthusian League desires to point out that the proposed scheme for the League of Nations has neglected to take account of the important questions of *the pressure of population*, which *causes the great international economic competition* and rivalry, and of the *increase of population*, which is put forward as a justification for *claiming increase of territory*. It, therefore, wishes to put on record its belief that the League of Nations will only be able to fulfill its aim *when it adds a clause* to the following effect:

"'That each Nation desiring to enter into the League of Nations shall pledge itself *so to restrict its birth rate* that its people shall be able to live in comfort *in their own dominions without need* for territorial expansion, and that it shall recognize that *increase of population shall not justify* a demand either for increase of territory or for the compulsion of other Nations to admit its emigrants; so that when all Nations in the League have shown their ability to live on their own resources without international rivalry, they will be in a position to fuse into an international federation, and territorial boundaries will then have little significance.'"

As a matter of course, the Peace Conference paid no attention to the resolution, for, as pointed out by Frank A. Vanderlip, the American financier, that conference not only ignored the economic factors of the world situaion, {*sic*} but seemed unaware that Europe had produced more people than its fields could feed. So the resolution amounted to so much propaganda and nothing more.

This remedy can be applied only by woman and she will apply it. She must and will see past the call of pretended patriotism and of glory of empire and perceive what is true and what is false in these things. She will discover what base uses the militarist and the exploiter make of the idealism of peoples. Under the clamor of the press, permeating the ravings of the jingoes, she will hear the voice of Napoleon, the archtype {*sic*} of the militarists of all nations, calling for "fodder for cannon."

"Woman is given to us that she may bear children," said he. "Woman is our property, we are not hers, because she produces children for us--we do not yield any to her. She is, therefore, our possession as the fruit tree is that of the gardener."

That is what the imperialist is thinking when he speaks of the glory of the empire and the prestige of the nation. Every country has its appeal--its shibboleth--ready for the lips of the imperialist. German rulers pointed to the comfort of the workers, to old-age pensions, maternal benefits and minimum wage regulations, and other material benefits, when they wished to inspire soldiers for the Fatherland. England's strongest argument, perhaps, was a certain phase of liberty which she guarantees her subjects, and the protection afforded them wherever they may go. France and the United States, too, have their appeals to the idealism of democracy--appeals which the politicians of both countries know well how to use, though the peoples of both lands are beginning to awake to the fact that their countries have been living on the glories of their revolutions and traditions, rather than the substance of freedom. Behind the boast of old-age pensions, material benefits and wage regulations, behind the bombast concerning liberty in this country and tyranny in that, behind all the slogans and shibboleths coined out of the ideals of the peoples for the uses of imperialism, woman must and will see the iron hand of that same imperialism, condemning women to breed and men to die for the will of the rulers.

Upon woman the burden and the horrors of war are heaviest. Her heart is the hardest wrung when the husband or the son comes home to be buried or to live a shattered wreck. Upon her devolve the extra tasks of filling out the ranks of workers in the war industries, in addition to caring for the children and replenishing the war-diminished population. Hers is the crushing weight and the sickening of soul. And it is out of her womb that those things proceed. When she sees what lies behind the glory and the horror, the boasting and the burden, and gets the vision, the human perspective, she will end war. She will kill war by the simple process of starving it to death. For she will refuse longer to produce the human food upon which the monster feeds.

CHAPTER XIV

WOMAN AND THE NEW MORALITY

UPON the shoulders of the woman conscious of her freedom rests the responsibility of creating a new sex morality. The vital difference between a morality thus created by women and the so-called morality of to-day, is that the new standard will be based upon knowledge and freedom while the old is founded upon ignorance and submission.

What part will birth control play in bringing forth this new standard? What effect will its practice have upon woman's moral development? Will it lift her to heights that she has not yet achieved, and if so, how? Why is the question of morality always raised by the objector to birth control? All these questions must be answered if we are to get a true picture of the relation of the feminine spirit to morals. They can best be answered by considering, first, the source of our present standard of sex morals and the reasons why those standards are what they are; and, second, the source and probable nature of the new morality.

We get most of our notions of sex morality from the Christian church--more particularly from the oldest existing Christian church, known as the Roman Catholic. The church has generally defined the "immoral woman" as one who mates out of wedlock Virtually, it lets it go at that. In its practical workings, there is nothing in the church code of morals to protect the woman, either from unwilling submission to the wishes of her husband, from undesired pregnancy, nor from any other of the outrages only too familiar to many married women. Nothing is said about the crime of bringing an unwanted child into the world, where often it cannot be adequately cared for and is, therefore, condemned to a life of misery. The church's one point of insistence is upon the right of itself to legalize marriage and to compel the woman to submit to whatever such marriage may bring. It is true that there are remedies of divorce in the case of the state, but the church has adhered strictly to the principle that marriage, once consummated, is indissoluble. Thus, in its operation, the church's code of sex morals has nothing to do with the basic sex rights of the woman, but enforces, rather, the assumed property rights of the man to the body and the services of his wife. They are man-made codes; their vital factor, as they apply to woman, is submission to the man.

Closely associated with and underlying the principle of submission, has been the doctrine that the sex life is in itself unclean. It follows, therefore, that all knowledge of the sex physiology or sex functions is also unclean and taboo. Upon this teaching has been founded woman's subjection by the church and, largely through the influence of the church, her subjection by the state to the needs of the man.

Let us see how these principles have affected the development of the present moral codes and some of their shifting standards. When we have finished this analysis, we shall know why objectors to birth control raise the "morality" question.

The church has sought to keep women ignorant upon the plea of keeping them "pure." To this end it has used the state as its moral policeman. Men have largely broken the grip of the ecclesiastics upon masculine education The ban upon geology and astronomy, because they refute the biblical version of the creation of the world, are no longer effective. Medicine, biology and the doctrine of evolution have won their way to recognition in spite of the united opposition of the clerics. So, too, has the right of woman to go unveiled, to be educated, and to speak from public platforms, been asserted in spite of the condemnations of the church, which denounced them as destructive of feminine purity. Only in sex matters has it succeeded in keeping the bugaboo alive.

It clings to this last stronghold of ignorance, knowing that woman free from sexual domination would produce a race spiritually free and strong enough to break the last of the bonds of intellectual darkness.

It is within the marriage bonds, rather than outside them, that the greatest immorality of men has been perpetrated. Church and state, through their canons and their laws, have encouraged this immorality.

It is here that the woman who is to win her way to the new morality will meet the most difficult part of her task of moral house cleaning.

In the days when the church was striving for supremacy, when it needed single-minded preachers, proselyters and teachers, it fastened upon its people the idea that all sexual union, in marriage or out of it, is sinful. That idea colors the doctrines of the Church of Rome and many other Christian denominations to this hour. "Marriage, even for the sake of children was a carnal indulgence" in earlier times, as Principal Donaldson points out in, "*The Position of Women Among the Early Christians*."[*] It was held that the child was "conceived in sin," and that as the result of the sex act, an unclean spirit had possession of it. This spirit can be removed only by baptism, and the Roman Catholic baptismal service even yet contains these words: "Go out of him, thou unclean spirit, and give place unto the Holy Spirit, the Paraclete."

In the *Intellectual Development of Europe*, John William Draper, speaking of the teaching of celibacy among the Early Fathers, says: "The sinfulness of the marriage relation and the preëminent value of chastity followed from their principles. If it was objected to such practices that by their universal adoption the human species would soon be extinguished and no man would remain to offer praises to God, these zealots, remembering the temptations from which they had escaped, with truth replied that there would always be sinners enough in the world to avoid that disaster, and that out of their evil work, good would be brought. Saint Jerome offers us the pregnant reflection that though it may be marriage that fills the earth, it is virginity that replenishes heaven."

The early church taught that there were enough children on earth. It needed missionaries more than it needed babies, and impressed upon its followers the idea that the birth wails of the infant were a protest against being born into so sordid a world.

Thus are we presented with one of the enormous inconsistencies of the church in sex matters. The teachings of the "Early Fathers" were effect the advocacy of an attempt to enforce birth control through absolute continence, while later it reverted, as it reverts to-day, to the Mosaic injunction to "be fruitful and multiply."

The very force of the sex urge in humanity compelled the church to abandon the teaching of celibacy for its general membership. Paul, who preferred to see Christians unmarried rather than married, had recognized the power of this force. In the seventh chapter of the First Epistle to the Corinthians (according to the Douay translation of the Vulgate, which is accepted by the Church of Rome), he said:

"8--But I say unto you the unmarried and the widows; it is good if they continue even as I.

"9--But if they do not contain themselves, let them marry, for it is better to marry than to be burnt."

When the church became a political power rather than a strictly religious institution, it needed a high birth rate to provide laymen to support its increasingly expensive organization.

It then began to exploit the sex force for its own interest. It reversed its position in regard to children. It encouraged marriage under its own control and exhorted women to bear as many children as possible. The world was just as sordid and the birth wails of the infants were just as piteous, but the needs of the hierarchy had changed. So it modified the standard of sex morality to suit its own requirements--marriage now became a sacrament.

Shrewd in changing its general policy from celibacy to marriage, the church was equally shrewd in perpetuating the doctrine of woman's subjection for its own interest. That doctrine was emphatically stated in the Third Chapter of the First Epistle of Peter and the Fifth Chapter of Paul's Epistle to the Ephesians. In the Douay version of the latter, we find this:

"22--Let women be subject to their husbands as to the Lord.

"23--Because the husband is the head of the wife; as Christ is the head of the Church.

"24--Therefore, as the Church is subject to Christ, so let the wives be to their husbands in all things."

These doctrines, together with the teaching that sex life is of itself unclean, formed the basis of morality as fixed by the Roman church.

Nor does the St. James version of the Bible, generally used by Protestant churches to-day, differ greatly in these particulars from the accepted Roman Catholic version, as a comparison will show.

If Christianity turned the clock of general progress back a thousand years, it turned back the clock two thousand years for woman. Its greatest outrage upon her was to forbid her to control the function of motherhood under any circumstances, thus limiting her life's work to bringing forth and rearing children. Coincident with this, the churchmen deprived her of her place in and before the courts, in the schools, in literature, art and society. They shut from her heart and her mind the knowledge of her love life and her reproductive functions. They chained her to the position into which they had thrust her, so that it is only after centuries of effort that she is even beginning to regain what was wrested from her.

"Christianity had no favorable effect upon, women," says Donaldson, "but tended to lower their character and contract the range of their activity. At the time when Christianity dawned upon the world, women had attained great freedom, power and influence in the Roman empire. Tradition was in favor of restriction, but by a concurrence of circumstances, women had been liberated from the enslaving fetters of the old legal forms. They enjoyed freedom of intercourse in society. They walked in the public thoroughfares with veils that did not hide their faces. They dined in the company of men. They studied literature and philosophy. They took part in political movements. They were allowed to defend their own law cases if they liked, and they helped their husbands in the government of provinces and the writing of books."

And again: "One would have imagined that Christianity would have favored the extension of woman's freedom. In a very short time women are seen only in two capacities--as martyrs and deaconesses (or nuns). Now what the early Christians did was to strike the male out of the definition of man, and human being out of the definition of woman. Man was a human being made to serve the highest and noblest purposes; woman was a female, made to serve only one."

Thus the position attained by women of Greece and Rome through the exercise of family limitation, and in a considerable degree of voluntary motherhood, was swept away by the rising tide of Christianity. It would seem that this pernicious result was premeditated, and that from the very early days of Christianity, there were among the hierarchy those who recognized the creative power of the feminine spirit, the force of which they sought to turn to their own uses. Certain it is that the hierarchy created about the whole love life of woman an atmosphere of degradation.

Fear and shame have stood as grim guardians against the gate of knowledge and constructive idealism. The sex life of women has been clouded in darkness, restrictive, repressive and morbid. Women have not had the opportunity to know themselves, nor have they been permitted to give play to their inner natures, that they might create a morality practical, idealistic and high for their own needs.

On the other hand, church and state have forbidden women to leave their legal mates, or to refuse to submit to the marital embrace, no matter how filthy, drunken, diseased or otherwise repulsive the man might be--no matter how much of a crime it might be to bring to birth a child by him.

Woman was and is condemned to a system under which the lawful rapes exceed the unlawful ones a million to one. She has had nothing to say as to whether she shall have strength sufficient to give a child a fair physical and mental start in life; she has had as little to do with determining whether her own body shall be wrecked by excessive childbearing. She has been adjured not to complain of the burden of caring for children she has not wanted. Only the married woman who has been constantly loved by the most understanding and considerate of husbands has escaped these horrors. Besides the wrongs done to women in marriage, those involved in promiscuity, infidelities and rapes become inconsequential in nature and in number.

Out of woman's inner nature, in rebellion against these conditions, is rising the new morality. Let it be realized that this creation of new sex ideals is a challenge to the church. Being a challenge to the church, it is also, in less degree, a challenge to the state. The woman who takes a fearless stand for the incoming sex ideals must expect to be assailed by reactionaries of every kind. Imperialists and exploiters will fight hardest in the open, but the ecclesiastic will fight longest in the dark. He understands the situation best of all; he best knows what reaction he has to fear from the morals of women who have attained liberty. For, be it repeated, the church has always known and feared the spiritual potentialities of woman's freedom.

And in this lies the answer to the question why the opponent of birth control raises the moral issue. Sex morals for women have been one-sided; they have been purely negative, inhibitory and repressive. They have been fixed by agencies which have sought to keep women enslaved; which have been determined, even as they are now, to use woman solely as an asset to the church, the state and the man. Any means of freedom which will enable women to live and think for themselves first, will be attacked as immoral by these selfish agencies.

What effect will the practice of birth control have upon woman's moral development? As we have seen in other chapters, it will break her bonds. It will free her to understand the cravings and soul needs of herself and other women. It will enable her to develop her love nature separate from and independent of her maternal nature.

It goes without saying that the woman whose children are desired and are of such number that she can not only give them adequate care but keep herself mentally and spiritually alive, as well as physically fit, can discharge her duties to her children much better than the overworked, broken and querulous mother of a large, unwanted family.

Thus the way is open to her for a twofold. development; first, through her own full rounded life, and next, through her loving, unstrained, full-hearted relationship with her offspring. The bloom of mother love will have an opportunity to infuse itself into her soul and make her, indeed, the fond, affectionate guardian of her offspring that sentiment now pictures her but hard facts deny her the privilege of being. She will preserve also her love life with her mate in its ripening perfection. She will want children with a deeper passion, and will love them with a far greater love.

In spite of the age-long teaching that sex life in itself is unclean, the world has been moving to a realization that a great love between a man and woman is a holy thing, freighted with great possibilities for spiritual growth. The fear of unwanted children removed, the assurance that she will have a sufficient amount of time in which to develop her love life to its greatest beauty, with its comradeship in many fields--these will lift woman by the very soaring quality of her innermost self to spiritual heights that few have attained. Then the coming of eagerly desired children will but enrich life in all its avenues, rather than enslave and impoverish it as do unwanted ones to-day.

What healthier grounds for the growth of sound morals could possibly exist than the ample spiritual life of the woman just depicted? Free to follow the feminine spirit, which dwells in the sanctuary of her nature, she will, in her daily life, give expression to that high idealism which is the fruit of that spirit when it is unhampered and unviolated. {p. 182} The love for her mate will flower in beauty of deeds that are pure because they are the natural expression of her physical, mental and spiritual being. The love for desired children will come to blossom in a spirituality that is high because it is free to reach the heights.

The moral force of woman's nature will be unchained--and of its own dynamic power will uplift her to a plane unimagined by those holding fast to the old standards of church morality. Love is the greatest force of the universe; freed of its bonds of submission and unwanted progeny, it will formulate and compel of its own nature observance to standards of purity far beyond the highest conception of the average moralist. The feminine spirit, animated by joyous, triumphant love, will make its own high tenets of morality. Free womanhood, out of the depths of its rich experiences, will observe and comply with the inner demands of its being. The manner in which it learns to do this best may be said to be the moral law of woman's being. So, in whatever words the new morality may ultimately be expressed, we can at least be sure that it will meet certain needs.

First of all, it will meet the physical and psychic requirements of the woman herself, for she cannot adequately perform the feminine functions until these are met. Second, it will meet the needs of the child to be conceived in a love which is eager to bring forth a new life, to be brought into a home where love and harmony prevail, a home in which proper preparation has been made for its coming.

This situation implies in turn a number of conditions. Foremost among them is woman's knowledge of her sexual nature, both in its physiology and its spiritual significance. She must not only know her own body, its care and its needs, but she must know the power of the sex force, its use, its abuse, as well as how to direct it for the benefit of the race. Thus she can transmit to her children an equipment that will enable them to break the bonds that have held humanity enslaved for ages.

To achieve this she must have a knowledge of birth control. She must also assert and maintain her right to refuse the marital embrace except when urged by her inner nature.

The truth makes free. Viewed in its true aspect, the very beauty and wonder of the creative impulse will make evident its essential purity. We will then instinctively idealize and keep holy that physical-spiritual expression which is the foundation of all human life, and in that conception of sex will the race be exalted.

What can we expect of offspring that are the result of "accidents"--who are brought into being undesired and in fear? What can we hope for from a morality that surrounds each physical union, for the woman, with an atmosphere of submission and shame? What can we say for a morality that leaves the husband at liberty to communicate to his wife a venereal disease?

Subversion of the sex urge to ulterior purposes has dragged it to the level of the gutter. Recognition of its true nature and purpose must lift the race to spiritual freedom. Out of our growing knowledge we are evolving new and saner ideas of life in general. Out of our increasing sex knowledge we shall evolve new ideals of sex. These ideals will spring from the innermost needs of women. They will serve these needs and express them. {p. 185} They will be the foundation of a moral code that will tend to make fruitful the impulse which is the source, the soul and the crowning glory of our sexual natures.

When women have raised the standards of sex ideals and purged the human mind of its unclean conception of sex, the fountain of the race will have been cleansed. Mothers will bring forth, in purity and in joy, a race that is morally and spiritually free.

CHAPTER XV

LEGISLATING WOMAN'S MORALS

ONE of the important duties before those women who are demanding birth control as a means to a New Race is the changing of our so-called obscenity laws. This will be no easy undertaking; it is usually much easier to enact statutes than to revise them. Laws are seldom exactly what they seem, rarely what their advocates claim for them. The "obscenity" statutes are particularly deceptive.

Enacted, avowedly, to protect society against the obscene and the lewd, they make no distinction between the scientific works of human emancipators like Forel and Ellis and printed matter such as they are ostensibly aimed at. Naturally enough, then, detectives and narow-minded {*sic*} judges and prosecutors who would chuckle over pictures that would make a clean-minded woman shudder, unite to suppress the scientific works and the birth-control treatises which would enable men and women to attain higher physical, mental, moral and spiritual standards.

Woman, bent upon her freedom and seeking to make a better world, will not permit the indecent and unclean forces of reaction to mask themselves forever behind the plea that it is necessary to keep her in ignorance to preserve her purity. In the birth-control movement, she has already begun to fight for her right to have, without legal interference, all knowledge pertaining to her sex nature. This is the third and most important of the epoch-making battles for general liberty upon American soil. It is most important because it is to purify the very fountain of the race and make the race completely free.

The first and most dramatic of the three great struggles for liberty reached its apex, as we know, in the American Revolution. It had for its object the right to hold such political beliefs as one might choose, and to act in accordance with those beliefs. If this political freedom is now lost to us, it is because we did not hold strongly enough to those liberties fought for by our forefathers.

Nearly a hundred years after the Revolution the battle for religious liberty came to a climax in the career of Robert G. Ingersoll. His championship of the much vaunted and little exercised freedom of religious opinion swept the blasphemy laws into the lumber room of outworn tyrannies. Those yet remaining upon the statute books are invoked but rarely, and then the effort to enforce them is ridiculous.

Within a few years the tragic combination of false moral standards and infamous obscenity laws will be as ridiculous in the public mind as are the now all but forgotten blasphemy laws. If the obscenity laws are not radically revised or repealed, few reactionaries will dare to face the public derision that will greet their attempts to use them to stay woman's progress.

The French have a saying concerning "mort main"--the dead hand. This hand of the past reaches up into the present to smother the rising flame of modern ideals, to reforge our chains when we have broken them, to arrest progress. It is the hand of such as have lived on earth but have not loved humanity. At the call of those who fear progress and freedom, it rises from the gloom of forgotten things to oppress the living.

It is the dead hand that holds imprisoned within the obscenity laws all direct information concerning birth control. It is the dead hand that thus compels millions of American women to remain in the bondage of maternity.

Previous to the year 1868, the obscenity laws of the various states in the Union contained no specific prohibition of information concerning contraceptives. In that year, however, the General

Assembly of New York passed an act which specifically included the subject of contraceptives. The act made it exactly as great an offense to give such information as to exhibit the sort of pictures and writings at which the legislation was ostensibly aimed.

In 1873, the late Anthony Comstock, who with a list of contributors, most of whom did not realize the real effects of his work, constituted the so-called Society for the Suppression of Vice, succeeded in obtaining the passage of the federal obscenity act. This act was presented as one to prevent the circulation of pornographic literature and pictures among school children. As such, it was rushed through with two hundred sixty other acts in the closing hours of the Congress. This act made it a crime to use the mails to convey contraceptives or information concerning contraceptives. Other acts later made the original law applicable to express companies and other common carriers, as well as to the mails.

With this precedent established--a precedent which a majority of the congressmen could hardly have understood because of the hasty passage of the act--Comstock secured the enactment of state laws to the same effect. Meanwhile, the provisions regarding contraceptives had been dropped from the amended New York State law of 1872. In 1873, however, a new section, said to have been drafted by Comstock himself, was substituted for the one enacted in 1872, and that section is essentially the substance of the present law. None of these acts made it an offense to prevent conception--all of them provided punishment for anyone disseminating information concerning the prevention of conception. In the federal statutes, the maximum penalties were fixed at a fine of $5,000 or five years imprisonment, or both. The usual maximum penalty under a state law is a fine of $1,000 or one year's imprisonment, or both.

Comstock has passed out of public notice. His body has been entombed but the evil that he did lives after him. His dead hand still reaches forth to keep the subject of prevention of conception where he placed it--in the same legal category with things unclean and vile. Forty years ago the laws were changed and the chief work of Comstock's life accomplished. Those laws still live, legal monuments to ignorance and to oppression. Through those laws reaches the dead hand to bring to the operating table each year hundreds of thousands of women who undergo the agony of abortion. Each year this hand reaches out to compel the birth of hundreds of thousands of infants who must die before they are twelve months old.

Like many laws upon our statute books, these are being persistently and intelligently violated. Few members of the well-to-do and wealthy classes think for a single moment of obeying them. They limit their families to one, two or three well-cared-for children. Usually the prosecutor who presents the case against a birth-control advocate, trapped by a detective hired by the Comstock Society, has no children at all or a small family. The family of the judge who passes upon the case is likely to be smaller still. The words "It is the law" sums it all up for these officials when they pass sentence in court. But these words, so magical to the official mind, have no weight when these same officials are adjusting their own private lives. They then obey the higher laws of their own beings--they break the obsolete statutes for themselves while enforcing them for others.

This is not the situation with the poorer people of the United States, however. Millions of them know nothing of reliable contraceptives. When women of the impoverished strata of society do not break these laws against contraceptives, they violate those laws of their inner beings which tell them not to bring children into the world to live in want, disease and general misery. They break the first law of nature, which is that of self preservation. {p. 193} Bound by false morals, enchained by false conceptions of religion, hindered by false laws, they endure until the pressure becomes so great that morals, religion and laws alike fail to restrain them. Then they for a brief respite resort to the surgeon's instruments.

For many years the semi-official witch hunting of the Comstock organization had a remarkable and a deadly effect. Everyone, whether it was novelist, essayist, publicist, propagandist or artist, who sought to throw definite light upon the forbidden subject of sex, or upon family limitation, was prosecuted if detected. Among the many books suppressed were works by physicians designed to warn young men and women away from the pitfalls of venereal diseases and sexual errors. The darkness that surrounded the whole field of sex was made as complete as possible.

Since then the feeling of the awakened women of America has intensified. The rapidity with which women are going into industry, the increasing hardship and poverty of the lower strata of society, the arousing of public conscience, have all operated to give force and volume to the demand for woman's right to control her own body that she may work out her own salvation.

Those who believe in strictly legal measures, as well as those who believe both in legal measures and in open defiance of these brutal and unjust laws, are demanding amendments to the obscenity statutes, which shall remove information concerning contraceptives from its present classification among things filthy and obscene.

An amendment typical of those offered is that drawn up for the New York statutes under the direction of Samuel McClure Lindsey, of Columbia University. The words and sentences in italics are those which it proposed to add:

(Section 1115.) Physicians' instruments *and information*. An article or instrument used or applied by physicians lawfully practicing, or by their direction or prescription, for the cure or prevention of disease, is not an article of indecent or immoral nature or use, within this article. The supplying of such articles to such physicians or by their direction or prescription, is not an offense under this article. *The giving by a duly licensed physician or registered nurse lawfully practicing, of information or advice in regard to, or the supplying to any person of any article or medicine for the prevention of, conception is not a violation of any provision of this article.*"

This proposed amendment should without doubt include midwives as well as nurses. There are thousands of women who never see a nurse or a physician. Under this section, even as it now stands, physicians have a right to prescribe contraceptives, but few of them have claimed that right or have even known that it has existed. It does exist, however, and was specifically declared by the New York State Court of Appeals, as we shall see when we consider that court's opinion in the Sanger case, farther on in the book. It can do no harm to make the intent of the law as regards physicians plainer, and it would be an immense step forward to include nurses and midwives in the section. With this addition it would remove one of the most serious obstacles to the freedom and advancement of American womanhood.

Every woman interested in the welfare of women in general should make it her business to agitate for such a change in the obscenity laws.

The above provision would take care of the case of the woman who is ill, or who is plainly about to become ill, but it does not take care of the vast body of women who have not yet ruined their health by childbearing and who are not yet suffering from diseases complicated by pregnancy. If this amendment had been attached to the laws in all the states, there would still remain much to be done.

Shall we go on indefinitely driving the now healthy mother of two children into the hands of the abortionist, where she goes in preference to constant ill health, overwork and the witnessing of dying and starving babies? It is each woman's duty to herself and to society to hasten the repeal of all laws against the communication of birth-control information. Now that she has the vote, she should use her political influence to strike, first of all, at these restrictive statutes. It is not to her credit that a district attorney, arguing against a birth control advocate, is able to show that women have made no effort to wipe out such laws in states where they have had the ballot for years.

It is time that women assert themselves upon this fundamental right, and the first and best use they can make of the ballot is in this direction. These laws were made by men and have been instruments of martyrdom and death for unnumbered thousands of women. Women now have the opportunity to sweep them into the trash heap. They will do it at once unless, like men, they use the ballot for those political honors which many years of experience have taught men to be hollow.

It is only a question of how long it will take women to make up their minds to this result. The law of woman's being is stronger than any statute, and the man-made law must sooner or later give way to it. Man has not protected woman in matters most vital to her--but she is awaking and will sooner or later realize this and assert herself. If she acts in mass now, it will be another cheering evidence that she is moving consciously toward her goal.

CHAPTER XVI

WHY NOT BIRTH-CONTROL CLINICS IN AMERICA

THE absurd cruelty of permitting thousands of women each year to go through abortions to prevent the aggravation of diseases for which they are under treatment assuredly cannot be much longer ignored by the medical profession. Responsibility for the inestimable damage done by the practice of permitting patients suffering from certain ailments to become pregnant, because of their ignorance of contraceptives, when the physician knows that if pregnancy goes to its full term it will hasten the disease and lead to the patient's death, must in all fairness be laid at his door.

What these diseases are and what dangers are involved in pregnancy are known to every practitioner of standing. Specialists have not been negligent in pointing out the situation.

[* This chapter, in substance, and largely in language, appeared under the present title in the March, 1920, issue of American Medicine (New York) and is incorporated in this book by courtesy of that publication.]

{p. 199} Eager to enhance or protect their reputations in the profession, they continually call out to one another: "Don't let the patient bear a child--don't let pregnancy continue."

The warning has been sounded most often, perhaps, in the cases of tubercular women. "In view of the fact that the tubercular process becomes exacerbated either during pregnancy or after childbirth, most authorities recommend that abortion be induced as a matter of routine in all tubercular women," says Dr. J. Whitridge Williams, obstetrician-in-chief to the Johns Hopkins Hospital, in his treatise on *Obstetrics*. Dr. Thomas Watts Eden, obstetrician and gynecologist to Charing Cross Hospital and member of the staffs of other notable British hospitals, extends but does not complete the list in this paragraph on page 652 of his *Practical Obstetrics*, "Certain of the conditions enumerated form absolute indications for the induction of abortion. These are nephritis, uncompensated valvular lesions of the heart, advanced tuberculosis, insanity, irremediable maligant tumors, hydatidiform mole, uncontrollable uterine hemorrhage, and acute hydramnios." We know that abortion, when performed by skilled hands, under right conditions, brings almost no danger to the life of the patient, and we also know that particular diseases can be more easily combatted after such an abortion than during a pregnancy allowed to come to full term. But why not adopt the easier, safer, less repulsive course and prevent conception altogether? Why put these thousands of women who each year undergo such abortions to the pain they entail and in whatever danger attends them?

Why continue to send home women to whom pregnancy is a grave danger with the futile advice: "Now don't get this way again!" They are sent back to husbands who have generations of passion and passion's claim to outlet. They are sent back without being given information as to how to prevent the dangerous pregnancy and are expected, presumably, to depend for their safety upon the husband's continence. The wife and husband are thrown together to bring about once more the same condition. Back comes the patient again in a few months to be aborted and told once more not to do it again.

Does any physician believe that the picture is overdrawn? I have known of many such cases. A recent one that came under my observation was that of a woman who suffered from a disease of the kidneys. Five times she was taken to a maternity hospital in an ambulance after falling in offices or in the street. One of the foremost gynecologists of America sent her out three times without giving her information as to the contraceptive means which would have prevented a repetition of this experience.

Why does this situation exist? We do not question the good intent nor the high purposes of these physicians. We know that they observe a high standard of ethics and that they are working for the uplift of the race. But here is a situation that is absurd -hideously absurd. What is the matter?

Several factors contribute to this state of affairs. First, the subject of contraception has been kept in the dark, even in medical colleges and in hospitals. Abortion has been openly discussed as a necessity under certain conditions, but the subject of contraception, as any physician will admit, has. not yet been brought to the front. It has escaped specialized attention in the laboratories and the research departments.

Thus there has been no professional stamp of approval by great bodies of experimenters. The result is that the average physician has felt that contraceptive methods are not yet established as certainties and has, for that reason, refused to direct their use.

Specialists are so busy with their own particular subjects and general practitioners are so taken up with their daily routine that they cannot give to the problem of contraception the attention it must have. Consultation rooms in charge of reputable physicians who have specialized in contraception, assisted by registered nurses--in a word, clinics designed for this specialty, would meet this crying need. Such clinics should deal with each woman individually, taking into account her particular disease, her temperament, her mentality and her condition, both physical and economic. Their sole function should be to prevent pregnancy. In accomplishing this purpose, a higher standard of hygiene is attained. Not only would a burden be removed from the physician who sends a woman to such a clinic, but there would be an improvement in the woman's general condition which would in a number of ways reflect itself in benefit to her family.

All this for the diseased woman. But every argument that can be made for preventive medicine can be made for birth-control clinics for the use of the woman who has not yet lost her health. Sound and vigorous at the time of her marriage, she could remain so if given advice as to by what means she could space her children and limit their number. When she is not given such information, she is plunged blindly into married life and a few years is likely to find her with a large family, herself diseased and damaged, an unfit breeder of the unfit, and still ignorant!

What are the fruits of this woeful ignorance in which women have been kept? First, a tremendous infant mortality--hundreds of thousands of babies dying annually of diseases which flourish in poverty and neglect.

Next, the rapid increase of the feebleminded, of criminal types and of the pathetic victims of toil in the child-labor factories. Another result is the familiar overcrowding of tenements, the forcing of the children into the street, the ensuing prostitution, alcoholism and almost universal physical and moral unfitness.

Those abhorrent conditions point to a blunder--upon the part of those to whom we have entrusted the care of the health of the individual, the family and the race. The medical profession, neglecting the principle involved in preventive medicine, has permitted these conditions to come about. If they were unavoidable, we should have to bear with them, but they are not unavoidable, as shown by facts and figures from other countries where contraceptive information is available.

In Holland, for instance, where the information concerning contraceptives has been accessible to the people, through clinics and pamphlets, since 1881, the general death rate and the infant mortality rate have fallen until they are the lowest in Europe. Amsterdam and The Hague have the lowest infant mortality rates of any cities in the world.

It is good to know that the first of the birth-control clinics of Holland followed shortly after a thorough and enthusiastic discussion of the subject at an international medical congress in Amsterdam in 1878. The Dutch Neo-Malthusian League was founded in 1881. The first birth-control clinic in the world was opened in 1885 by Dr. Aletta Jacobs in Amsterdam. So great were the results obtained that there has been a remarkable increase in the wealth, stamina, stature and longevity of the people, as well as a gradual increase in the population.

These clinics must not be confused with the white enameled rooms which we associate with the term in America. They are ordinary offices with the necessary equipment, or rooms in the homes of the nurses, fitted out for the work. They are places for consultation and examination, opened by specially trained nurses who have been instructed by Dr. J. Rutgers, of The Hague, secretary of the Neo-Malthusian League, who has devoted his life to this work. There have been more than fifty nurses trained specially for this work by Dr. Rutgers. As a nurse completes her course of training, she establishes herself in a community and her place of consultation is called a clinic.

The general results of this service are best judged by tables included in the *Annual Summary of Marriages, Births and Deaths in England, Wales, Etc.*, for 1912.[*]

In Amsterdam, the birth rate dropped from 37.1 for the period of 1881-85 to 24.7 for 1906 and 23.3 in 1912. During the same periods, the death rate fell from 25.1 to 13.1, and in 1912 to 11.2. Infant mortality for the same period fell from 203 for each thousand living births to 90, and in 1912 to 64. Illegitimate fertility also decreased. Results in other cities, as shown by the table at the end of this chapter, are exactly similar.

In the Australian Commonwealth, where birth control is taken as a matter of course, and information concerning contraceptives is available to the masses, the births were so well distributed in 1915 that while the birth rate was 27.3, there was an infant death rate of only 10.7. New Zealand, which is also one of the typical birth-control countries, had a birth rate of 25.3 and an infant death rate of only 9.1 for the same year. These figures are in marked and happy contrast with those for the birth registration of the United States, where the reports for 1916 show a birth rate of 24.9, but an infant death rate of 14.7. A similar comparison may be made with the German Empire in 1913., where there was a birth rate of 27.5 in 1913 and an infant mortality rate of 15. In these countries, birth control information is not so generally within the reach of the masses and, consequently, the largest percentage of births come to that class least able to bring children to full maturity, as indicated in the infant mortality rates.

In conclusion, I am going to make a statement which may at first seem exaggerated, but which is, nevertheless, carefully considered. The effort toward racial progress that is being made to-day by the medical profession, by social workers, by the various charitable and philanthropic organizations and by state institutions for the physically and mentally unfit, is practically wasted. All these forces are in a very emphatic sense marking time. They will continue to mark time until the medical profession recognizes the fact that the ever increasing tide of the unfit is overwhelming all that these agencies are doing for society.

They will continue to mark time until they get at the source of these destructive conditions and apply a fundamental remedy. That remedy is birth control.

* Amsterdam [Malthusian (Birth Control) League started 1881; Dr. Aletta Jacobs gave advice to poor women, 1885]:

	1881-85	1906-10	1912
Birth rate	37.1	27.7	23.3 per 1,000 of population
Death rate	25.1	13.1	11.2 per 1,000 of population
INFANTILE MORTALITY: Deaths in first year	203	90	64 per thousand living births

The Hague [now headquarters of the Neo-Malthusian (Birth Control) League]:

	1881-85	1906-10	1912
Birth rate	38.7	27.5	23.6 per 1,000 of population
Death rate	23.3	13.2	10.9 per 1,000 of population
INFANTILE MORTALITY: Deaths in first year	214	99	66 per thousand living births

These figures are the lowest in the whole list of death rates and infantile mortalities in the summary of births and deaths in cities in this report.

Rotterdam:

	1881-85	1906-10	1912
Birth rate	37.4	32.0	29.0 per 1,000 of population
Death rate	24.2	13.4	11.3 per 1,000 of population
INFANTILE MORTALITY:	209	105	79 per thousand living

Deaths in first year   births

Fertility and Illegitimacy Rates:

	1880-2	1890-2	1900-2	
egitimate fertility	306.4	296.5	252.7	Legitimate births per married women aged 45.

	1880-2	1890-2	1900-2	
egitimate fertility	16.1	16.3	11.31	Illegitimate births per unmarried women, age to 45.

The Hague:

	1880-2	1890-2	1900-2
egitimate fertility	346.5	303.9	255.0
egitimate fertility	13.4	13.6	7.7

Rotterdam:

	1880-2	1890-2	1900-2
egitimate fertility	331.4	312.9	299.0
egitimate fertility	17.4	16.5	13.1

CHAPTER XVII

PROGRESS WE HAVE MADE

THE silence of the centuries has been broken. The wrongs of woman and the rights of woman have found voices. These voices differ from all others that have been raised in woman's behalf. They are not the individual protests of great feminine minds, nor the masculine remedies for masculine oppression suggested by the stricken consciences of a few men. Great voices are heard, both of women and of men, but intermingled with them are millions of voices demanding freedom.

Let it be repeated that movements mothered by emancipated women are often deceptive in character. The demand for suffrage, the agitation against child labor, the regulation of working hours for women, the insistence upon mothers' pensions are palliatives all. Yet as woman's understanding develops and she learns to think at the urgence of her own inner nature, rather than at the dictates of men she moves on from these palliatives to fundamental remedies. So at the crest of the wave of woman's revolt comes the movement for voluntary motherhood--not a separate, isolated movement, but the manifestation of a cosmic force--the force that moves the wave itself.

The walls of the cloister have fallen before the cries of a rising womanhood. The barriers of prurient puritanism are being demolished. Free woman has torn the veil of indecency from the secrets of life to reveal them in their power and their purity. Womanhood yet bound has beheld and understood. A public whose thoughts and opinions had been governed by men and by women engulfed in the old order has been shocked awake.

Sneers and jests at birth control are giving way to a reverent understanding of the needs of woman. They who to-day deny the right of a woman to control her own body speak with the hardihood of invincible ignorance or with the folly of those blind ones who in all ages have opposed the light of progress. Few there are to insist openly that woman remain a passive instrument of reproduction. The subject of birth control is being lifted out of the mire into which it was cast by puritanism and given its proper place among the sciences and the ideals of this generation. With this effort has come an illumination of all other social problems. Society is beginning to give ear to the promise of modern womanhood: "When you have ceased to chain me, I shall by the virtue of a free motherhood remake the world."

It would be miraculous indeed if that victory which has been won, had been gained without great toil, insufferable anguish and sacrifice such as all persons experience when they dare to brave the conventions of the dead past or blaze a trail for a new order.

But where the vision is clear, the faith deep, forces unseen rally to assist and carry one over barriers which would otherwise have been insurmountable. No part of this wave of woman's emancipation has won its way without such vision and faith.

This is the one movement in which pioneering was unnecessary. The cry for deliverance always goes up. It is its own pioneer. The facts have always stared us in the face. No one who has worked among women can be ignorant of them. I remember that ever since I was a child, the idea of large families associated itself with poverty in my mind. As I grew to womanhood, and found myself working in hospitals and in the homes of the rich and the poor, the association between the two ideas grew stronger.

In every home of the poor, women asked me the same question. As far back as 1900, 1 began to inquire of my associates among the nurses what one could tell these worried women who asked constantly: "What can I do?" It is the voice of the elemental urge of woman--it has always been there; and whether we have heeded it or neglected it, we have always beard it. Out of this cry came the birth control movement.

Economic conditions have naturally made this elemental need more plain; sometimes they have lent a more desperate voice to woman's cry for freedom. Men and women have arisen since Knowlton and Robert Dale Owen, to advocate the use of contraceptives, but aside from these two none has come forward to separate it from other issues of *sex* freedom. But the birth control movement as a movement for woman's *basic* freedom was born of that unceasing cry of the socially repressed, spiritually stifled woman who is constantly demanding: "What can I do to avoid more children?"

When it came time to arouse new public interest in birth control and organize a movement, it was found expedient to employ direct and drastic methods to awaken a slumbering public. The Woman Rebel, a monthly magazine, was established to proclaim the gospel of revolt. When its mission was accomplished and the words "birth control" were on their way to be a symbol of woman's freedom in all civilized tongues, it went out of existence.

The deceptive "obscenity law," invoked oftener to repress womanhood and smother scientific knowledge than to restrain the distribution of verbal and pictorial pornography, was deliberately challenged. This course had two purposes. It challenged the constitutionality of the law and thereby brought knowledge of contraceptives to hundreds of thousands of women.

The first general, organized effort reached in various ways to all parts of the United States. Particular attention was paid to the mining districts of West Virginia and Montana, the mill towns of New England and the cotton districts of the Southern states. Men and. women from all these districts welcomed the movement. They sent letters pledging their loyalty and their active assistance. They participated directly and indirectly in the protest, which awakened the country.

As time went on, the work was extended to various foreign elements of the population, this being made possible by the enthusiastic cooperation of workers who speak the foreign languages.

Leagues were formed to organize those who favored changing the laws. Lectures were delivered throughout the United States. Articles were written by eminent physicians, scientists, reformers and revolutionists. Debates were arranged. Newspapers and magazines of all kinds, classes and languages gave the subject of birth control serious attention, taking one side or the other of the discussion that was aroused. New books on the subject began to appear. Books by foreign authors were reprinted and distributed in the United States. The Birth Control Review, edited by voluntary effort and supported by a stock company of women who make contributions instead of taking dividends, was founded and continues its work.

After a year's study in foreign countries for the purpose of supplementing the knowledge gained in my fourteen years as a nurse, I came back to the United States determined to open a clinic. I had decided that there could be no better way of demonstrating to the public the necessity of birth control and the welcome it would receive than by taking the knowledge of contraceptive methods directly to those who most needed it.

A clinic was opened in Brooklyn. There 480 women received information before the police closed the consulting rooms and arrested Ethel Byrne, a registered nurse, Fania Mindell, a translator, and myself. The purpose of this clinic was to demonstrate to the public the practicability and the necessity of such institutions. All women who came seeking information were workingmen's wives. All had children. No unmarried girls came at all. Men came whose wives had nursing children and could not come. Women came from the farther parts of Long island, from cities in Massachusetts and Connecticut and even more distant places. Mothers brought their married daughters. Some whose ages were from 25 to 35 looked fifty, but the clinic gave them new hope to face the years ahead. These women invariably expressed their love for children, but voiced a common plea for means to avoid others, in order that they might give sufficient care to those already born. They wanted them "to grow up decent."

For ten days the two rooms of this clinic were crowded to their utmost. Then came the police. We were hauled. off to jail and eventually convicted of a "crime."

Ethel Byrne instituted a hunger strike for eleven days, which attracted attention throughout the nation. It brought to public notice the fact that women were ready to die for the principle of voluntary motherhood. So strong was the sentiment evoked that Governor Whitman pardoned Mrs. Byrne.

No single act of self-sacrifice in the history of the birth-control movement has done more to awaken the conscience of the public or to arouse the courage of women, than did Ethel Byrne's deed of uncompromising resentment at the outrage of jailing women who were attempting to disseminate knowledge which would emancipate the motherhood of America.

Courage like hers and like that of others who have undergone arrest and imprisonment, or who night after night and day after day have faced street crowds to speak or to sell literature--the faith and the untiring labors of still others who have not come into public notice--have given the movement its dauntless character and assure the final victory.

One dismal fact had become clear long before the Brownsville clinic was opened. The medical profession as a whole had ignored the tragic cry of womanhood for relief from forced maternity. The private practitioners, one after another, shook their heads and replied: "It cannot be done. It is against the law," and the same answer came from clinics and public hospitals.

The decision of the New York State Court of Appeals has disposed of that objection, however, though as yet few physicians have cared to make public the fact that they take advantage of the decision. While the decision of the lower courts in my own case was upheld, partly because I was a nurse and not a physician, the court incidentally held that under the laws as they now stand in New York, any physician has a right to impart information concerning contraceptives to women as a measure for curing or preventing disease. The United States Supreme Court threw out my appeal without consideration of the merits of the case. Therefore, the decision of the New York State Court of Appeals stands. And under that decision, a physician has a right, and it is therefore his duty, to prescribe contraceptives in such cases, at least, as those involving disease.

It is true that Section 1142 of the Penal Code of New York State does not except the medical man, and does not allow him to instruct his patient in birth control methods, even though she is suffering from tuberculosis, syphilis, kidney disorders or heart disease. Without looking farther, the physicians had let that section go at its face value. No doctor had questioned either its purpose or its legal scope. The medical profession was content to let this apparent limitation upon its rights stand, and it remained for a woman to go to jail to demonstrate the fact that under another section of the same code--1145--the physician had the vital right just described.

It is safe to say that many physicians do not even yet know of their legal rights in this matter.

But here is what the New York State Court of Appeals said on Janury {*sic*} 8, 1918, in an opinion thus far unquestioned and which is the law of the state:

"Secondly, by section 1145 of the Penal Law, physicians are excepted from the provisions of this act under circumstances therein mentioned. This section reads: 'An article or instrument, used or applied by physicians lawfully practicing, or by their direction or prescription, for the cure or prevention of disease, is not an article of indecent or immoral nature or use, within this article. The supplying of such articles to such physicians or by their direction or prescription, is not an offense under this article."

"This exception in behalf of physicians does not permit advertisements regarding such matters, nor promiscuous advice to patients irrespective of their condition, but it is broad enough to protect the physician who in good faith gives such advice to a married help person to cure or prevent disease. 'Disease,' by Webster's International Dictionary, is defined to be, 'an alteration in the state of the body, or of some of its organs, interrupting or disturbing the performance of the vital functions, and causing or threatening pain and sickness; illness, disorder.'

"The protection thus afforded the physician would also extend to the druggist, or vendor, acting upon the physician's prescription or order."

Section 1142, which shamelessly classes contraceptive information with abortion and things obscene, still stands, but under the decision of the Court of Appeals, it is the law of New York State that physicians have the right which they were seemingly denied. Such is probably the fact, also, in many other states, for the so-called "obscenity" laws are modelled more or less, after the same pattern. One of the chief results of the Brownsville clinic was that of establishing for physicians a right which they neglected to establish for themselves, but which they are bound, in the very nature of things, to exercise to an increasing degree. Similar tests by women in other states would doubtless establish the right elsewhere in America.

We know of some thirty-five arrests of women and men who have dared entrenched prejudice and the law to further the cause of birth control. The persistent work in behalf of the movement, attended as it was by danger of fines and jail sentences, seemed to puzzle the authorities. Sometimes they dismissed the arrested persons, sometimes they fined them, somtimes {*sic*} they imprisoned them. But the protests went on, and through these self-sacrifices, word of the movement went constantly to more and more people.

Each of these arrests brought added publicity. Each became a center of local agitation. Each brought a part of the public, at least, face to face with the issue between the women of America and this barbarous law.

Many thousands of letters have been answered and thousands of women have been given personal consultations. Each letter and each consultation means another center of influence from which the gospel of voluntary motherhood spreads.

Forced thus to the front, the problems of birth control and the right of voluntary motherhood have been brought more and more to the attention of medical students, nurses, midwives, physicians, scientists and sociologists. A new literature, ranging all the way from discussion of the means of preventing conception to the social, political, ethical, moral and spiritual possibilities of birth control, is coming into being. Women's cry for liberty is infusing itself into the thoughts and the consciences and the aspirations of the intellectual leaders as well into the idealism of society.

It is but a few years since it was said of The Woman Rebel that it was "the first unveiled head raised in America." It is but a few years since men as well as women trembled at the temerity of a public discussion in which the subject of sex was mentioned.

But, measured in progress, it is a far cry from those days. The public has read of birth control on the first page of its newspapers. It has discussed it in meetings and in clubs. It has been a favorite topic of discussion at correct teas. The scientist is giving it reverent and profound attention. Even the minister, seeking to keep abreast of the times, proclaims it from the pulpit. And everywhere, serious-minded women and men, those with the vision, with a comprehension of present and future needs of society, are working to bring this message to those who have not yet realized its immense and regenerating import.

The American public, in a word, has been permeated with the message of birth control. Its reaction to that message has been exceedingly encouraging. People by the thousands have flocked to the meetings. Only the official mind, serving ancient prejudices under the cloak of "law and order," has been in opposition.

It is plain that puritanism is in the throes of a lingering death. If anyone doubts it, let it be remembered that the same people who, a few years ago, formed the official opinion of puritanism have so far forsaken puritanism as to flood the country with millions of pamphlets discussing sex matters and venereal disease. This literature was distributed by the United States Government, by state governments, by the Y.M.C.A, the Y.W.C.A, and by similar organizations. It treated the physiology of sex far more definitely than has birth-control literature. This official educational barrage was at once a splendid salute to the right of women and men to know their own bodies and the last heavy firing in the main battle against ignorance in the field of sex. What remains now is but to take advantage of the victories.

What does it all mean? It means that American womanhood is blasting its way through the débris of crumbling moral and religious systems toward freedom. It means that woman has but to press on, more courageously, more confidently, with her face set more firmly toward the goal.

CHAPTER XVIII

THE GOAL

WHAT is the goal of woman's upward struggle? Is it voluntary motherhood? Is it general freedom? Or is it the birth of a new race? For freedom is not fruitless, but prolific of higher things. Being the most sacred aspect of woman's freedom, voluntary motherhood is motherhood in its highest and holiest form. It is motherhood unchained--motherhood ready to obey its own urge to remake the world.

Voluntary motherhood implies a new morality--a vigorous, constructive, liberated morality. That morality will, first of all, prevent the submergence of womanhood into motherhood. It will set its face against the conversion of women into mechanical maternity and toward the creation of a new race.

Woman's rôle has been that of an incubator and little more. She has given birth to an incubated race. She has given to her children what little she was permitted to give, but of herself, of her personality, almost nothing. In the mass, she has brought forth quantity, not quality. The requirement of a male dominated civilization has been numbers. She has met that requirement.

It is the essential function of voluntary motherhood to choose its own mate, to determine the time of childbearing and to regulate strictly the number of offspring. Natural affection upon her part, instead of selection dictated by social or economic advantage, will give her a better fatherhood for her children. The exercise of her right to decide how many children she will have and when she shall have them will procure for her the time necessary to the development of other faculties than that of reproduction. She will give play to her tastes, her talents and her ambitions. She will become a full-rounded human being.

Thus and only thus will woman be able to transmit to her offspring those qualities which make for a greater race.

The importance of developing these qualities in the mothers for transmission to the children is apparent when we recall certain well-established principles of biology. In all of the animal species below the human, motherhood has a clearly discernible superiority over fatherhood. It is the first pulse of organic life. Fatherhood is the fertilizing element. Its development, compared to that of the mother cell, is comparatively new. Likewise, its influence upon the progeny is comparatively small. There are weighty authorities who assert that through the female alone comes those modifications of form, capacity and ability which constitute evolutionary progress. It was the mothers who first developed cunning in chase, ingenuity in escaping enemies, skill in obtaining food, and adaptability. It was they also who attained unfailing discretion in leadership, adaptation to environment and boldness in attack. When the animal kingdom as a whole is surveyed, these stand out as distinctly feminine traits. They stand out also as the characteristics by which the progress of species is measured.

Why is all this true of the lower species yet not true of human beings? The secret is revealed by one significant fact--the female's functions in these animal species are not limited to motherhood alone. Every organ and faculty is fully employed and perfected. Through the development of the individual mother, better and higher types of animals are produced and carried forward. In a word, natural law makes the female the expression and the conveyor of racial efficiency.

Birth control itself, often denounced as a violation of natural law, is nothing more or less than the facilitation of the process of weeding out the unfit, of preventing the birth of defectives or of those who will become defectives. So, in compliance with nature's working plan, we must permit womanhood its full development before we can expect of it efficient motherhood. If we are to make racial progress, this development of womanhood must precede motherhood in every individual woman. Then and then only can the mother cease to be an incubator and be a mother indeed. Then only can she transmit to her sons and daughters the, qualities which make strong individuals and,, collectively, a strong race.

Voluntary motherhood also implies the right of marriage without maternity. Two utterly different functions are developed in the two relationships. In order to give the mate relationship its full and free play, it is necessary that no woman should be a mother against her, will. There are other reasons, of course--reasons more frequently emphasized--but the reason just mentioned should never be overlooked. It is as important to the race as to the woman, for through it is developed that high love impulse which, conveyed to the child, attunes and perfects its being.

Marriage, quite aside from parentage, also gives two people invaluable experience. When parentage follows in its proper time, it is a better parentage because of the mutual adjustment and development--because of the knowledge thus gained. Few couples are fitted to understand the sacred mystery of child life until they have solved some of the problems arising out of their own love lives.

Maternal love, which usually follows upon a happy, satisfying mate love, becomes a strong and urgent craving. It then exists for two powerful, creative functions. First, for its own sake, and then for the sake of further enriching the conjugal relationship. It is from such soil that the new life should spring. It is the inherent right of the new life to have its inception in such physical ground, in such in spiritual atmosphere. The child thus born is indeed a flower of love and tremendous joy. It has within it the seeds of courage and of power. This child will have the greatest strength to surmount hardships, to withstand tyrannies, to set still higher the mark of human achievement.

Shall we pause here to speak again of the rights of womanhood, in itself and of itself, to be absolutely free? We have talked of this right so much in these pages, only to learn that in the end, a free womanhood turns of its own desire to a free and happy motherhood, a motherhood which does not submerge the woman, but which is enriched because she is unsubmerged. When we voice, then, the necessity of setting the feminine spirit utterly and absolutely free, thought turns naturally not to rights of the woman, nor indeed of the mother, but to the rights of the child--of all children in the world. For this is the miracle of free womanhood, that in its freedom it becomes the race mother and opens its heart in fruitful affection for humanity.

How narrow, how pitifully puny has become motherhood in its chains! The modern motherhood enfolds one or two adoring children of its own blood, and cherishes, protects and loves them. It does not reach out to all children. When motherhood is a high privilege, not a sordid, slavish requirement, it will encircle all. Its deep, passionate intensity will overflow the limits of blood relationship. Its beauty will shine upon all, for its beauty is of the soul, whose power of enfoldment is unbounded.

When motherhood becomes the fruit of a deep yearning, not the result of ignorance or accident, its children will become the foundation of a new race. There will be no killing of babies in the womb by abortion, nor through neglect in foundling homes, nor will there be infanticide. Neither will children die by inches in mills and factories. No man will dare to break a child's life upon the wheel of toil.

Voluntary motherhood will not be passive, resigned, or weak. Out of its craving will come forth a fierceness of love for its fruits that will make such men as remain un awakened stand aghast at its fury when offended. The tigress is less terrible in defense of her offspring than will be the human mother. The daughters of such women will not be given over to injustice and to prostitution; the sons will not perish in industry nor upon the battle field. Nor could they meet these all too common fates if an undaunted motherhood were there to defend. Childhood and youth will be too valuable in the eyes of society to waste them in the murderous mills of blind greed and hate.

This is the dawn. Womanhood shakes off its bondage. It asserts its right to be free. In its freedom, its thoughts turn to the race. Like begets like. We gather perfect fruit from perfect trees. The race is but the amplification of its mother body, the multiplication of flesh habitations-- beautified and perfected for souls akin to the mother soul.

The relentless efforts of reactionary authority to suppress the message of birth control and of voluntary motherhood are futile. The powers of reaction cannot now prevent the feminine spirit from breaking its bonds. When the last fetter falls the evils that have resulted from the suppression of woman's will to freedom will pass. Child slavery, prostitution, feeblemindedness, physical deterioration, hunger, oppression and war will disappear from the earth.

In their subjection women have not been brave enough, strong enough, pure enough to bring forth great sons and daughters. Abused soil brings forth stunted growths. An abused motherhood has brought forth a low order of humanity. Great beings come forth at the call of high desire. Fearless motherhood goes out in love and passion for justice to all mankind. It brings forth fruits after its own kind. When the womb becomes fruitful through the desire of an aspiring love, another Newton will come forth to unlock further the secrets of the earth and the stars. There will come a Plato who will be understood, a Socrates who will drink no hemlock, and a Jesus who will not die upon the cross. These and the race that is to be in America await upon a motherhood that is to be sacred because it is free

Advertisements from first edition